THE SIMPLICITY OF GOD

CASCADE COMPANIONS

The Christian theological tradition provides an embarrassment of riches: from Scripture to modern scholarship, we are blessed with a vast and complex theological inheritance. And yet this feast of traditional riches is too frequently inaccessible to the general reader.

The Cascade Companions series addresses the challenge by publishing books that combine academic rigor with broad appeal and readability. They aim to introduce nonspecialist readers to that vital storehouse of authors, documents, themes, histories, arguments, and movements that comprise this heritage with brief yet compelling volumes.

RECENT TITLES IN THIS SERIES:

Cascade Companion to Evil by Charles Taliaferro
Metaphysics by Donald Wallenfang
Phenomenology by Donald Wallenfang
Virtue by Olli-Pekka Vainio
Reading Paul by Michael Gorman
The Rule of Faith by Everett Ferguson
The Second-Century Apologists by Alvyn Pettersen
Origen by Ronald E. Heine
Athanasius of Alexandria by Lois Farag
Practicing Lament by Rebekah Eklund
Forgiveness: A Theology by Anthony Bash
Called to Attraction: The Theology of Beauty by Brendan T. Sammon
A Primer in Ecotheology by Celia Deane-Drummond
Postmodern Theology by Carl Raschke
Jacques Ellul by Jacob E. Van Vleet and Jacob M. Rollinson
Understanding Pannenberg by Anthony C. Thiselton
The Becoming of God: Process Theology by Ronald Faber
Theology and Science Fiction by James F. McGrath
The U.S. Immigration Crisis by Miguel de la Torre
Feminism and Christianity by Caryn Riswold
Queer Theology by Linn Marie Tonstad

THE SIMPLICITY OF GOD

A Theological Invitation

JONATHAN M. PLATTER

CASCADE *Books* • Eugene, Oregon

THE SIMPLICITY OF GOD: A THEOLOGICAL INVITATION

Cascade Companions

Copyright © 2025 Jonathan M. Platter. All rights reserved. Except for brief quotations in critical publications or reviews, no part of this book may be reproduced in any manner without prior written permission from the publisher. Write: Permissions, Wipf and Stock Publishers, 199 W. 8th Ave., Suite 3, Eugene, OR 97401.

Cascade Books
An Imprint of Wipf and Stock Publishers
199 W. 8th Ave., Suite 3
Eugene, OR 97401

www.wipfandstock.com

PAPERBACK ISBN: 979-8-3852-2396-1
HARDCOVER ISBN: 979-8-3852-2397-8
EBOOK ISBN: 979-8-3852-2398-5

Cataloguing-in-Publication data:

Names: Platter, Jonathan M., author.

Title: The simplicity of God : a theological invitation / Jonathan M. Platter.

Description: Eugene, OR : Cascade Books, 2025 | Series: Cascade Companions | Includes bibliographical references and index.

Identifiers: ISBN 979-8-3852-2396-1 (paperback) | ISBN 979-8-3852-2397-8 (hardcover) | ISBN 979-8-3852-2398-5 (ebook)

Subjects: LCSH: Thomas, Aquinas, Saint, 1225?–1274. | God (Christianity)—Simplicity—History of doctrines. | God (Christianity)—Attributes. | God (Christianity)—Immutability. | God (Christianity)—History of doctrines.

Classification: BT148 .P55 2025 (paperback) | BT148 (ebook)
09/09/25

Unless otherwise specified, Scripture quotations are taken from the New Revised Standard Version Updated Edition. Copyright © 2021 National Council of Churches of Christ in the United States of America. Used by permission. All rights reserved worldwide. https://www.friendshippress.org/pages/about-the-nrsvue

For Janette, Julian, and Hildie

CONTENTS

Figures | ix

Acknowledgments | xi

Abbreviations | xv

Introduction | xvii

PART I: THE IDEA OF DIVINE SIMPLICITY | 1

1 What Is God? On Persisting in Asking Unanswerable Questions | 3

2 The Grammar of God-Talk: Simplicity as "Depth-Grammar" | 13

3 Describing the Divine: Simplicity as Metaphysics | 23

4 Being and Naming: Simplicity, Scripture, and Language for God | 49

PART II: EXPERIMENTS IN CHRISTIAN DOCTRINE | 71

5 Trinity | 73

6 Creation | 99

7 Incarnation | 117

8 Eschatology | 138

Conclusion: God Whose Giving Knows No Ending | 157

Bibliography | 161

General Index | 175

Scripture Index | 181

FIGURES

Figure 5.1 — Lessons from the Variations of Rahner's Rule | 82

Figure 7.1 — Chart of the Four Major Christological Heresies | 121

Figure 7.2 — *Communicatio idiomatum* (Communication of Attributes) | 130

ACKNOWLEDGMENTS

THE THEME OF THIS book has been a passion of mine for the last ten years, when I began reading Hans Urs von Balthasar under the mentorship of Steve McCormick. I will always be grateful for his friendship and encouragement. Since those first encounters, I've been privileged with more theological friendships and people willing to read and discuss my work than I deserve. Matthew Codd and Jacob Lett have been consistent dialogue partners over the last decade; the shape of my thinking would be quite different without the gift of their friendship, and this book has benefited from their comments on several sections. I am grateful for the mentoring and now friendship of my *Doktorvater*, Ian McFarland, who has influenced my work and thinking in numerous ways. Simeon Zahl has been a significant encouragement, and his questions before I even began this project have accompanied me throughout, as have those of Christoph Schwöbel, whose unexpected death in 2021 was a major loss.

Kurt Knecht read the book in its entirety (some of it multiple times); it has benefited greatly from his careful editorial eye and perceptive theological comments. Renee Dutter Miller also provided comments on several chapters and was a dialogue partner for me throughout the writing.

Acknowledgments

My TA, Leah Taylor, read and discussed early drafts of several chapters. Her notes improved the overall clarity and raised questions that informed the rest of the writing. Additionally, I was supported, encouraged, and challenged through discussion with Dawn Araujo-Hawkins, Vern Barnet, Christina Bohn, Andy Cook, Don Compier, Scott Dermer, Fr. Steven King, Noah Murdoch, Brinna Ream, and Mtr. Brittany Sparrow-Savage, as well as my parents and siblings: Paul, Joan, Cori, David, Joshua, and Hannah.

The germs of this project took shape under the funding of the *Exzellenzinitiative*. I'm grateful for a postdoctoral fellowship (winter 2021–2022) with the Catholic Faculty of Theology at LMU Munich (Ludwig-Maximilians Universität), and especially to Thomas Schärtl for his generous hospitality and dialogue. A paper containing material that has now been integrated into chapters 2 and 3 was presented at the *Oberseminar* led by Prof. Schärtl. The engagement of all present informed my revisions and adaptation. While I'm indebted to readers and dialogue partners for whatever virtues this book might possess, I alone am responsible for its errors and shortcomings.

I wouldn't have had the time to write this book without the support of my department chair, Scott Dermer, and VPAA, Abby Hodges. They helped me adjust my teaching schedule for fall 2024 so that I could carve out time for writing. Thanks are due as well to Mark Hayse in the library for securing resources, and to Glenda Seifert for assisting me with numerous interlibrary loans. Thanks also to Debra Bradshaw of the William Broadhurst Library at Nazarene Theological Seminary for access to their wonderful resources. The entire team at Wipf and Stock Publishers provided prompt and clear guidance throughout the project.

My in-laws, Perry and Dallis Parker, helped me secure lodging in Dallas, Texas, for one week in spring 2023 to

Acknowledgments

develop the initial plans and prospects for this book, but the time and arrangements for this stay only came about because my wife, Janette, encouraged me to get some time away during the break. As with many other things over the last decade and a half, this book would likely never have come to fruition without Janette's love and support. I dedicate this book to her with our children, Julian and Hildie—the three people in whose love I know something of the love God is.

Christmastide 2024

ABBREVIATIONS

ANF	*Ante-Nicene Fathers*. Edited by Alexander Roberts and James Donaldson.
Bicentennial	*The Bicentennial Edition of the Works of John Wesley* (1960–).
CD	Barth, Karl. *Church Dogmatics*.
Jackson	*The Works of John Wesley* (1872). Edited by Thomas Jackson.
NJPS	New Jewish Publication Society translation of the Hebrew Bible (*Tanakh*)
NKJV	New King James Version
NPNF2	*Nicene and Post-Nicene Fathers*, Second Series. Edited by Philip Schaff and Henry Wace.
NRSVue	New Revised Standard Version Updated Edition
PG	Patrologia Graeca = Patrologiae Cursus Completus: Series Graeca. Edited by Jacques-Paul Migne.
PL	Patrologia Latina = Patrologiae Cursus Completus: Series Latina. Edited by Jacques-Paul Migne.
ScG	Thomas Aquinas. *Summa contra Gentiles*.
ST	Thomas Aquinas. *Summa Theologiae*.

For premodern and early modern sources, references to text locations are provided in Arabic numerals, based on the divisions in the work. For example, Augustine, *City of God*, 11.10.1 refers to Book 11, Chapter 10, paragraph 1. In the case of Augustine's *On the Trinity*, I omit chapter numbers, because they differ in some translations while the paragraph numbers are continuous throughout each Book; so Augustine, *Trinity*, 8.10 refers to Book 8, Paragraph 10. Aquinas, *Summa Theologiae*, 1.2.2 refers to Prima Pars (First Part), Question 2, Article 2. I occasionally alter translations of foreign-language sources, and I indicate this in the citation with "alt." If I provide my own translation, this is noted in the citation as well, with citation of the original-language source. Quotations from the Greek of the New Testament are from the SBL Greek text.

INTRODUCTION

IN HIS BIOGRAPHY OF St. Thomas Aquinas, G. K. Chesterton explains his omission of commentary on Aquinas's theology:

> A lady I know picked up a book of selections from St. Thomas with a commentary; and began hopefully to read a section with the innocent heading, "The Simplicity of God." She then laid down the book with a sigh and said, "Well, if that's His simplicity, I wonder what His complexity is like." With all respect to that excellent Thomistic commentary, I have no desire to have this book laid down, at the very first glance, with a similar sigh.[1]

Chesterton's story suggests a bleak prospect for an entire book on the simplicity of God. If God is simple, why does it take so many words to explain?

The Christian creedal tradition is committed to the idea that God is in some sense "one," for the Nicene Creed confesses belief in *one God* and states that Father, Son, and Spirit are "of one nature" or "consubstantial" (Greek: *homoousion*). At its core, simplicity is a way of articulating the oneness and unity of God: God's unity is a distinctive kind of unity, consisting of no parts whatsoever. Not even the

1. Chesterton, *St. Thomas Aquinas*, "Introductory Note."

triune persons are "parts" of God, because if they were, none of them would *be* God but rather only *a* part (one-third?) of God.[2] So God's unity doesn't seem to be a part-whole unity (i.e., a "composite" unity, made up of real parts).

Divine simplicity has benefited from renewed interest, but its reception has been mixed and often isolated to narrow academic confines. No small part of the problem is the steep cost of entry to understand the basic meaning and motivation of divine simplicity (Chesterton's anecdote is plausible). The remainder of the book strains at the task of introducing the *meaning* of simplicity. But below the surface, occasionally irrupting into the text, is a more fundamental desire to convey something of the *motivation*, the pathos, and the integral spiritual vision underlying even philosophically dense expositions of simplicity. What is this integral spiritual vision? What's the deeper motivation for thinking of God as "simple"?

There's not a single (simple?) way to put it, but many: It's Julian of Norwich's account of Christ our Mother (Luke 13:34), in whose kindness our "kind" are joined to God's self.[3] It's Hildegard of Bingen's vision of the blazing fire of God engulfing all and suffusing all with divine energy.[4] It's Thomas Aquinas's resistance to knowing anything more than that God "is"—and that even this seemingly simplistic thought contains riches.[5] It's Sarah Coakley's articulation of the mystery of prayer—of being incorporated into the Spirit's unifying life, that hospitable love by which our loves

---

2. See Platter, *Divine Simplicity and the Triune Identity*, 23–26.

3. Julian, *Revelations*, Long Text, §58–59. On the multiple resonances of "kindness" in Julian's writings, see Soskice, *Kindness of God*, 1–6.

4. Hildegard, *Scivias*, 2.1.

5. Aquinas, *Summa Theologiae*, 1.2.2; 1.3.4; 1.13.11 (from now on cited as *ST*).

are redeemed.⁶ While these theologians aren't all saying the same thing, there seems to be a cohesive grammar that connects them: something like a mystical apprehension of God as the depth dimension of existence.

Evelyn Underhill (1875–1941) captures this grammar succinctly, suggesting that the mystical apprehension of God as "simple" is driven by a desire to "know the real." In her words, "Mysticism is the art of union with Reality." As she recognizes, this is no easy or obvious task; instead, it prods the would-be mystic to ask a challenging question, "*What is Reality?*—a question, perhaps, which never occurred to him before . . . and he knows that it will cause him infinite distress."⁷ She expands on this, saying,

> Reality . . . is pure creative Life. . . . Union with reality—apprehension of it—will upon this hypothesis be union with life at its most intense point: in its most dynamic aspect. . . . Beauty, Goodness, Splendour, Love, all those shining words which exhilarate the soul, are but the names of aspects or qualities picked out by human intuition as characteristic of this intense and eternal Life.⁸

Apprehending God as "simple" is driven by a passionate commitment to "knowing the real," where such knowing is a form of *intimacy* with a more encompassing reality rather than the possession of discrete "facts."

There is a depth to reality, and abiding in this depth requires an open-ended attention to that which is not directly known—to an "ever-greater" reality. "God" is not just a name for some already known being, another person I

---

6. Coakley, *God, Sexuality, Self*, 111–15; and Coakley, *New Asceticism*, 85–100.

7. Underhill, *Practical Mysticism*, 3.

8. Underhill, *Mysticism*, 29, 30.

Introduction

can sometimes cozy up to and sometimes step away from. That would make God out to be *a* reality, rather than *the* reality. But how might one know God if God is such a "depth" of reality? This is the question that sustains the Christian life, never settled by a formula or technique. Rather, this question has its "answer" only in forming a whole life, participating in the movement of this ever-greater God toward wholeness, reconciliation, and liberation.

And yet, part of the theologian's task is to speak about this very God without reducing God to lifeless concepts. This is the theological vocation of every believer, not just academic theologians and ordained clergy. Such a task requires careful speech and a mode of language that is consistently attentive to its intrinsic limitations. Is there a way to talk about God when we risk replacing God with an idol every time we open our mouths? In this book, I'm inviting you to consider divine simplicity through this kind of lens: simplicity is a kind of God-talk that is also an orienting guide to God-appropriate God-talk.[9]

These convictions underlie Part I, "The Idea of Simplicity." The first chapter directly invokes this abiding question in one of its many forms: *What is God?* The next two chapters follow up on the unanswerability of this question, first by articulating the linguistic constraints theology faces ("the grammar of God-talk") and then imagining how our descriptive and "metaphysical" concepts are to be transformed for use with God ("describing the divine"). The last chapter of Part I makes good on the promise that God-talk really is possible, even though the mode of this talk is unique. We best approach God through many *names* (chapter 4), which remains a fraught and risky business but matches scripture's doxological mode of address.

---

9. Similarly, see Long, *Perfectly Simple Triune God*, xix–xxvi.

Introduction

Part II, "Explorations in Christian Doctrine," is more exploratory and could be read in alternative orderings as the reader sees fit. Here, I test the approach developed in Part I with four doctrines: Trinity, creation, incarnation, and eschatology. If we take "simplicity" as a direct description of God, it is problematic for each of these doctrines— and I try to face the difficulties directly. But I argue that if we approach simplicity through the integrated account developed in Part I, simplicity generates rich possibilities for doctrinal construction.

This is, then, an unapologetically *theological* introduction to divine simplicity. While I try to engage responsibly with the contributions from philosophers of religion, my purpose is not to induct readers into that philosophical discourse. Rather, *doctrine* is the end goal, particularly insofar as doctrine is an activity internal to the life of faith.[10] God is, to riff on Anselm (1033–1109), that than which nothing more radically unique can be thought.[11] But this is bound to the good news that God is radically *pro nobis* (for us). The God who is incomparably unique (i.e., "simple") is also incomparably intimate by active love and self-gift.

---

10. Cf. "Homily on Psalm 115," §1, in Basil the Great, *On Christian Doctrine and Practice*, 218–19, who grounds right speech and right belief in the life of faith, though his emphasis on "unquestioning faith" seems overstated.

11. The original quotation, from Anselm's *Proslogion*, §2, and known for its role in the "ontological proof," says God is "that than which nothing greater can be thought"; in *Major Works*, 87.

PART I
THE IDEA OF DIVINE SIMPLICITY

1

WHAT IS GOD?

On Persisting in Asking Unanswerable Questions

> It should please [us] to count as nothing everything that is made, in order to have the love of God who is unmade. For this is the reason why those who deliberately occupy themselves in earthly business, and are constantly seeking worldly success, find no peace from this in heart or soul: because they love and seek rest here in this thing which is so small and in which there is no rest, and do not know God, who is almighty, all wise, and all good, for he is true rest.
>
> —JULIAN OF NORWICH[1]

---

1. Julian, *Revelations*, Short Text, §8.

PART I: THE IDEA OF DIVINE SIMPLICITY

IN AN EPISODE OF *Brooklyn Nine-Nine*, an American sitcom about a team of detectives in a fictional precinct of New York City, Sergeant Jeffords is trying to log into the computer of Captain Raymond Holt, his commanding officer, to access a file in the captain's absence.[2] The show presents Captain Holt as a cultured, highly rational, and stoic character; Sergeant Jeffords is a muscular-yet-emotional family-man who's easily flustered. Not knowing the captain's password, Sergeant Jeffords attempts to answer the security questions. He presses "forgot password," confidently prepares to breeze through the security process, and is then confronted with an unexpected question: *What is God?* After what appears to have been a long study session, another detective asks how it's going; he responds in exasperation, "Not good! I'm reading this book on religion, and apparently there's some debate as to what God is!"

Although we shouldn't expect to need an answer to this question to resolve IT problems, this scene is at least a reminder of how perplexing this question really is. That's not only the case because there really are debates about how to answer the question, but also because the question itself doesn't naturally come up in ordinary Christian experience. Even amongst theologians and religious scholars, we've become accustomed to asking a different question in its place, preferring to ask "*who* God is" rather than "*what* God is." Because the doctrine of divine simplicity has its home within a tradition that does ask the "what" question and we, on the other hand, are accustomed to dropping that question altogether, many of us never even seriously consider whether God is "simple."

So what does it mean to affirm (or deny) that God is simple? To clarify the idea of God as simple, I start with the question that stumped Sergeant Jeffords: *What is God?* By

2. Lampassi, *Brooklyn Nine-Nine*.

thinking about how someone like St. Thomas Aquinas persisted in asking this question (even if it can't be answered), we can get a sense of the role simplicity plays. After this initial introduction, I discuss two different roles simplicity plays in Christian theology, what I call the "grammatical" and the "metaphysical." I show that some theologians prefer to think of simplicity purely in terms of one role or the other, though there might be good reasons to integrate the grammatical and metaphysical with one another. Thinking about these different functions will set us up to interpret various biblical arguments and images for simplicity in chapter 4, as well as provide some tools for navigating the debates discussed in Part II.

QUID SIT DEUS?: THE QUESTION OF DIVINE SIMPLICITY

The doctrine of divine simplicity is given paradigmatic expression by St. Augustine (354–430 CE) when he says that God *is* what God *has*.[3] Augustine's expression is repeated throughout Christian history—as St. Hildegard of Bingen (1098–1179) puts it, "whatever is in God is God."[4] In claiming that God is all that God has, simplicity is a *denial* that there are more basic elements out of which God is composed or into which God could be divided up. From another, perhaps more fundamental angle, however, it is the *affirmation* of God's total ontological otherness. "The distinction" between God and creation goes all the way to the level of being (for present purposes, saying that the otherness is "ontological" is to say that it's not only a difference according to appearance or our mode of knowledge but is a difference at the level of "being"). We could say that in both

3. Augustine, *City of God*, 11.10.1.
4. Hildegard, *Selected Writings*, 21.

senses divine simplicity pertains to asking, "What is God?" (in Aquinas's Latin: *Quid sit Deus?*). When inquiring about what God is, one potential answer is "God is all that God has, without more basic pieces," and equally we could say, "God is creation's ontological Other." However, it's worth noting that treating these expressions as straightforward answers to the question is misleading. The first (if given as a definition of God) is practically a tautology, like Karl Barth's (1886–1968) early expression "God is God."[5] Rather than providing an actual definition of God, this answer *evades* definition by saying that God is nothing other than God. The second, although phrased as an affirmation, is at base also a negation: whatever God is, God is not whatever created reality is.

In this way, we might be able to see why St. Thomas Aquinas (1225–1274) can in almost the same breath ask what God is, deny that we can give an answer, and then proceed to a number of weighty affirmation-like statements, such as God *is* simple, *is* being itself, *is* self-subsisting existence. We misunderstand Aquinas if we assume that in asking *quid sit* and denying the possibility of an answer he is simply engaged in an artificially modest act of throat-clearing, as if to say "Yes, yes, I know we can't 'know' what God is, but really, I've got this." Aquinas means it when he asks the question and then says we can't answer it. He is saying that we need to hold in mind this unanswerable question to avoid collapsing God into creation or thinking of God by too direct an analogy with creation.

---

5. Barth, *Epistle to the Romans*. However, Robert Jenson interprets the "is" in this phrase as a transitive active verb, making the "tautology" less tautologous (*Story and Promise*, 119–20). Rendered this way, "God *is* God" means something like "God *enacts* God" or *God is an event that "happens" purely by virtue of God's action.*

This becomes clear when we see what Aquinas says he's up to in the "five ways" to the existence of God (sometimes referred to as the "five proofs").[6] Placed near the beginning of the *Summa Theologiae*, the "five ways" are now widely discussed as philosophical proofs of the existence of God. The five ways are: (1) the argument from motion, (2) the argument from efficient causation, (3) the argument from possibility and necessity, (4) the argument from degrees of perfection, and (5) the argument from goal-directedness. Aquinas's aim, however, is not exactly to *prove* beyond doubt that God exists, but to defend the idea of theology as a "science"—that is, a meaningful intellectual activity oriented to a specific object of study. The problem for Aquinas is that if we cannot define "what God is," then "theology" doesn't have a properly specified object of investigation and therefore can't be called a "science."[7] And yet, according to Aquinas, theology *is* a science because it does know how to specify its object *even if that object is incapable of being defined*.[8] Theology knows how to specify its object of investigation because the word "God" has a consistent *use* in relation to the limits of what we can understand about the created world (even if God has no technical, metaphysical definition).[9] That is to say, no matter how we slice up the world—whether, for example, according to how things get into motion (first way) or according to the orientation of things to their completion/fulfillment (fifth way)—there

---

6. Aquinas, *ST*, 1.2.3. Citations of Aquinas's *Summa Theologiae* typically refer to the Response (where Aquinas's own views are expressed), unless I specify a reply to a particular objection (e.g., "ad 1," would mean "reply to objection 1").

7. Aquinas, *ST*, 1.1.7, ad 1; 1.3, intro.

8. Aquinas, *ST*, 1.2.2, ad 2.

9. Cf. Placher, *Domestication of Transcendence*, 22–26; Burrell, *Aquinas*, 7–8.

are edges of meaning or comprehension, ways in which our thinking tends toward nonsense apart from a commitment to creation's dependency on God. In this sense, Aquinas and Barth are closer than is sometimes recognized. They both understand the first theological task to consist in attending to the unique reality of God, rather than providing foundations for belief in God or affirming a generic religious experience.[10]

Aquinas alerts readers to the limits of our ability to conceive the world by introducing the constant threat of infinite regresses, which shows that our thinking about ordinary experiences of motion, causation, possibility, gradation in perfection, and fulfillment only carries on successfully by dependence on a higher order of speculation—a higher "science" or what David Burrell calls "depth grammar."[11] Theology is a "science" because theology has to do with "God," by which we mean (among other things) that which enables the success of all other sciences and produces the beauty of all other beings without being reducible to one member in that order of reality or identified with the sum of all created beings.

PERSISTING IN ASKING UNANSWERABLE QUESTIONS

That is to say, theology persists in asking what God is (*quid sit Deus*) to remind us that God is *not* what any creature is nor the sum of all creatures. Or, we persist in asking to remind us of our inability to have the final answer. In Barth's Kierkegaard-inspired expression, it is to say that God is the Wholly Other—and this is not a description of

10. Barth, *Church Dogmatics*, esp. vols. I/1 and II/1. Hereafter, cited as *CD*.

11. Burrell, *Aquinas*.

God but an insistence on the inaccessibility and uncontrollability of God: God is not at our disposal.[12] In Aquinas's terms, we can get a preliminary sense of how this plays out by looking at his vexing expression that in God "essence is not distinct from existence . . . his essence, therefore, *is* his existence," whereas in creatures essence and existence are really distinct.[13] This is central to Aquinas's articulation of divine simplicity. Part of his reasoning for saying this is his vision of the dependence of all really existing beings on the generous act of God to grant them existence. For Aquinas, creating is a continuous act by which God donates existence by unceasingly granting to that which is not God participation in God's own excess of being.[14] A creature's essence (the *kind* of being it is) does not account for its existence (the *fact that* the creature exists). When we ask "what is that creature?" we can answer the question straightforwardly, and yet that question brings us no closer to understanding how it is that that creature came to exist and continues to exist (which, according to the doctrine of creation from nothing, is only answerable by reference to God the Creator and not by reference to something intrinsic to the creature).

I've said that we persist in asking *what God is* to remind us of what God is *not*: neither another creaturely being nor the sum of all creaturely beings. Now I'm claiming that the same logic leads Aquinas to say that in God essence and existence are identical: God has existence and is

---

12. *CD*, IV/1, 186. Here Barth explicitly denies that "Wholly Other" can serve as a governing description of God, because it's normed instead by the actual presence of God in Christ—so for Barth the expression is a christologically normed insistence on the freedom of God.

13. Aquinas, *ST*, 1.3.4 (my translation); and Aquinas, *On Being and Essence*, C4, §78–80.

14. For interpretation, see Davison, *Participation in God*, 113–31; McFarland, *From Nothing*, 85–98; and Oliver, *Creation*, 43–53.

the kind of being that God ineffably is (that is, the one and only God) in a manner that is completely incommensurate with created beings. Thinking in terms of how it is that something exists, this means that God *is* God's existence whereas creatures *receive* existence. God exists because "to exist" is intrinsic to what and who God is. God simply *is* the dynamic plenitude of actuality and goodness that, by God's free act of love and generosity, overflows and exceeds any kind of private self-possession by evoking the participation of that which has no reality in itself. God invites the created other into the beauty of God's abundant life—an abundance known partially in the simple fact of existing, and an abundance perfected in us at the consummation of all things when God is "all in all" (1 Cor 15:28). By attending to the distinction between God and creation, Aquinas comes to an affirmation of the simplicity of God—the unbounded identity of essence and existence, that God is all that God has. This too is another way of saying that we can't answer the *what* question, at least not in a straightforward manner, since to comprehend God's essence would require comprehending God's existence (because Aquinas makes them identical), and no one can comprehend God (Exod 33:20; Ps 145:3; Job 26:14; Eph 4:6).

Already two kinds of language have shown up in working out the simultaneous value and unanswerability of the question of *what God is*. On the one hand, I've relied on the language of difference and otherness between God and creatures ("the distinction"), and on the other hand I've introduced the more metaphysical language of essence and existence, identical in God but distinct in creatures. I've suggested that the second, metaphysical language as used by Aquinas can be seen as another way of expressing the denial that God is identifiable as one being among others or as the sum of all creatures. However, it's worth thinking about the ways that these two forms of approaching divine simplicity don't always overlap so neatly. Some theologians prefer to give preference (either relatively or absolutely) to one or the other. Some insist that divine simplicity is only a way to regulate our language in order to avoid idolatry (the idolatry of reducing God to creaturely status by thinking our language is more adequate to God than it really is), which I discuss as the "grammar of God-talk." While others develop a more conceptually elaborate picture of God's simplicity by drawing on metaphysical categories, which I discuss as the "metaphysics of divine being." Although they don't have to be opposed, recognizing the distinction can help to make sense of how simplicity plays different roles for different theologians, and the distinction can also clarify how some critics of simplicity have taken it too strictly as an exemplar of either "grammar" or "metaphysics." These are the subjects of the next two chapters.

I don't expect this discussion would be of much help to *Brooklyn Nine-Nine*'s Sergeant Jeffords as he's trying to answer a password security question. But hopefully it helps us as we think about the role the question "what is God?" has had in Christian theology and how the question provides an initial context for divine simplicity. Can we say what God is? I prefer to side with Aquinas here: we need to persist in asking, but the question itself is unanswerable. Still, asking the question with the knowledge that it cannot be answered does not leave us with nothing to say, nor does it invalidate the task of theology (as though we're stuck chasing our tails). On the contrary, it pushes us to find further ways to express the excessive, abundant, and generous God whose triune life encompasses our own lives without collapsing us into mere puppets of God's designs or reducing

PART I: THE IDEA OF DIVINE SIMPLICITY

God to a pantheistic sum of the parts. Divine simplicity is a way of holding this all together: (1) the need to remember that God is *not* what any creature is and (2) the affirmation of the generous and intimate outpouring of God's love—which is the outpouring of God's own self for us—as the genuine self-disclosure and self-gift of God's nature.

QUESTIONS

1. This chapter distinguishes between two questions for the doctrine of God: the *who* and the *what* questions. Which question do you tend to start with? Are they both equally important?

2. This chapter suggests that the question of *what* God is can't be answered. Do you agree or disagree? Why or why not?

3. Can you think of additional biblical passages that affirm God's incomprehensibility? Any that seem to suggest we *can* know what God is?

2

THE GRAMMAR OF GOD-TALK

Simplicity as "Depth-Grammar"

God is full and whole and beyond the beginning of time, and therefore he cannot be divided or analysed by words as a human being can. God is a whole and nothing other than a whole, to which nothing can be added and from which nothing can be taken away. . . . But God is fullness and whatever is in God is God. God cannot be shaken or passed through a sieve by human thinking, for there isn't anything in God that is not God.

—HILDEGARD OF BINGEN[1]

THE IDEA THAT THEOLOGY is concerned with shaping our language (that is, with "grammar") and not merely with

---

1. "Letter to Odo of Soissons," in Hildegard, *Selected Writings*, 21.

describing divine matters is not new in theology. Among the first Christian theologians following the apostolic age, Irenaeus of Lyons (c. 130–202 CE) employs a metaphor of Scripture as a mosaic. His gnostic opponents have put the pieces together poorly, so that what should display an artfully depicted king is instead a badly executed image of a dog, which the gnostics then parade as though the image were in fact of the king. The problem is not simply that Irenaeus's opponents had described the matter incorrectly or that they had drawn from the wrong sources; rather, the problem is that "by violently drawing away from their proper connection, words, expressions, and parables whenever found, [they] adapt the oracles of God to their baseless fictions."[2] In contrast, Irenaeus commends the "rule of faith," a kind of creed in outline that guides Christian reading of Scripture and reception of the apostolic witness to ensure that Christians continue to testify, in thought and worship, to their proper "king," God the Father who, with the two hands Jesus and the Spirit, creates, sustains, redeems, and fulfills all creation.[3]

In Irenaeus's view, the rule of faith is a hermeneutical guide for both understanding Scripture and producing faithful speech. It is like a "grammar" for rightly understanding God in Scripture. As controversies continue to spur the church's conceptual refinement of their shared confession, theologians have continued to explore the way this grammatical understanding of theology—that is, theology as passing on the rule of faith—affects the very activity of using language and its idolatrous potential. This is especially evident in debates in which the Cappadocians find themselves involved in the wake of the Council

2. Irenaeus, *Against Heresies*, 1.8.1 (*ANF* 1:326).

3. Irenaeus, *Against Heresies*, 3.4.1–2, 4.33.7–8 (*ANF* 1:416–17, 508).

of Nicaea, especially Basil of Caesarea (c. 330–79) and his younger brother Gregory of Nyssa (c. 335–95). While all debate partners were committed to the idea of creation out of nothing, Basil and Gregory were bolder about how our language for God is affected by the radical difference creation out of nothing expresses between God and creation.[4] As Gregory develops the implications of this distinction, he notes a pervasive factor of all language that is problematic when one turns to speak of God, namely that our language is used for things that are "spaced" or "gappy" (from the Greek root *diastema*, meaning something like "interval" or "gap") and extended through space and time. But God is without such extension and consists of no spaced components.[5] Creaturely existence is so thoroughly "spaced" that even our language is spaced and keeps our thinking directed to extended and spaced realities. When we turn to speak of God, we are attempting in our "spaced" thoughts and language to articulate the one who is beyond such spacing.[6] Consequently, we have to try to think better than we can speak—we try to keep in check the ways our language unwittingly spaces out God. In this sense, to say God is simple—beyond the spacing that spaces out finite things—is to provide a grammatical rule for theology: avoid speaking of God in ways that assume our spaced language for God rightly depicts God as though God were in reality so spaced.

---

4. For some discussion of how this common commitment to *creatio ex nihilo* mixed with other factors surrounding Nicaea, see Anatolios, *Retrieving Nicaea*, 36–41.

5. Gregory of Nyssa, *Contra Eunomium*, 1:135, 184–85 (*NPNF*2 5:144, 215). This aspect of Gregory's thought was brought to prominence especially in the pioneering study of von Balthasar, *Presence and Thought*, 48, 156, 166.

6. Gregory of Nyssa, "Homily 7," 125.

PART I: THE IDEA OF DIVINE SIMPLICITY

WITTGENSTEIN, LINDBECK, AND (POSTLIBERAL) GRAMMATICAL THEOLOGY

We've already seen how Aquinas used the question *quid sit Deus* to provide a kind of grammatical role for simplicity (ch. 1). In contemporary theology, the grammatical function of doctrine has been given new prominence, especially with the advent of postliberalism and through dialogue with the early-twentieth-century philosopher Ludwig Wittgenstein (1889–1951).[7] Wittgenstein initiated the "linguistic turn" in philosophy by suggesting that many of the conventional problems of philosophy could be deflated by a proper understanding of how language works.[8] Wittgenstein argues that language is rooted in the "forms of life" within which it's used, so it has more to do with human *action* than with mere description. In our daily lives, we're always *doing* things, and language only has meaning within the context of this activity. Meaning is found in context-specific use of words for context-specific purposes—Wittgenstein calls this a "language game."[9] Language games carry their own set of commitments and aims and generate a particular interpretive and affective posture toward the world. For Wittgenstein, we are likely to create unnecessary problems for ourselves if we assume our language is only functioning descriptively or as if its primary function was to put nametags on objects. Consequently, philosophy should often work in a therapeutic mode—offering corrective treatment for malformed patterns of thought and speech.

7. Lindbeck, *Nature of Doctrine*; and Kerr, *Theology After Wittgenstein*.

8. Wittgenstein, *Philosophical Investigations*, §38. I cite *Philosophical Investigations* by paragraph/section number. Citations are from Part I unless Part II is specified (in some editions, Part II is called "Philosophy of Psychology—A Fragment").

9. Wittgenstein, *Philosophical Investigations*, §23.

George Lindbeck (1923–2018), in his landmark book *The Nature of Doctrine: Religion and Theology in a Postliberal Age*, adopted Wittgenstein's approach to language to rethink the function of doctrine and, ultimately, to open up new possibilities for ecumenical dialogue.[10] Lindbeck calls this a "cultural-linguistic" model of doctrine. Religion and theology, he suggests, are culturally embedded and ritually enacted language games—i.e., symbol systems that "structure human experience and understanding of self and world" especially when such a language game takes "interest in the maximally important."[11] A religion is a whole cultural-linguistic reality, a story that gives a comprehensive interpretive scheme for navigating the world in relation to that which is "maximally important." Such a story, Lindbeck says, "is not primarily a set of propositions to be believed, but is rather the medium in which one moves, a set of skills that one employs in living one's life."[12] Lindbeck draws an analogy between the saint and a skilled poet like Homer, suggesting that the saint's religiosity is like an "interiorized skill." That is, "it is like the grammatical or rhetorical knowledge of a poet such as Homer, who could not enunciate a single rule in either discipline [viz., grammar or rhetoric] and yet was able to sense as could no one else what conformed or did not conform to the spirit, the unarticulated rules, of the Greek language."[13] Theology, on this view, is "grammar"—that is, it's the task of articulating formal rules for how the speech proper to Christian worship, proclamation, and formation works.[14]

---

10. First published in 1984; anniversary edition published in 2009 (edition used here).

11. Lindbeck, *Nature of Doctrine*, 18.

12. Lindbeck, *Nature of Doctrine*, 21.

13. Lindbeck, *Nature of Doctrine*, 22.

14. Lindbeck, *Nature of Doctrine*, 65–70.

PART I: THE IDEA OF DIVINE SIMPLICITY

DIVINE SIMPLICITY AS GRAMMAR

In terms of divine simplicity, a grammatical approach would say that divine simplicity is a rule for avoiding speech about God that is idolatrous because it confuses God with the being of creatures. In this sense, we might think of divine simplicity as a summary of the task initiated by simultaneously *asking* after the essence or "whatness" of God and denying that the asking will reach a determinative end. It is to say that we ask after God's quiddity to avoid thinking of God in the way we think of creatures.

David Burrell's (1933–2023) work pioneered a new approach to interpreting Aquinas's arguments in the early questions of the *Summa Theologiae* that is sometimes referred to as "grammatical Thomism." My own discussion of Aquinas in chapter 1 is indebted to Burrell's early book, *Aquinas: God and Action*.[15] Burrell suggests that we misunderstand the early questions of the *Summa* if we take them as descriptions of God, words that refer to God or the divine nature in a picture-building way. Instead, Burrell's Aquinas is engaged first in theological "depth grammar"—that is, investigation of the background assumptions that make theological activity possible. The common influence of Wittgenstein's philosophy of language results in some overlap between the "cultural-linguistic" view of doctrine proposed by Lindbeck (published a few years after Burrell's *Aquinas*) and Burrell's grammatical interpretation of Aquinas. In particular, both emphasize the *function* of language and its embeddedness in particular cultural practices and forms of life, and both emphasize the "skill" aspect of religious and theological activity. But we also see the repetition of a theme from Gregory of Nyssa concerning the need to

---

15. First published in 1979; third edition published in 2016 (edition used here).

The Grammar of God-Talk

use language to express what is beyond the power proper to our language: "Aquinas is concerned to *show* what we cannot use our language to say, yet there is no medium of exposition available other than language itself."[16] So how do we get our language to "show" what it cannot say? How can we use our language faithfully to speak of a God who is indefinable? Burrell identifies two strategies in Aquinas.

First, theological depth grammar is attentive to the formal features of our language and is sensitive to how different domains of inquiry might require the development of different formal features. One such formal feature is "compositeness" (the quality of being composed/composite) which our language naturally expresses due to its own subject–predicate form. This is a way our language functions that's inherent in its form—that's what it means to be a "formal feature." Our language is transparent to the structure of finite things, because the compositeness of our language fits the compositeness of the things we talk about. For example, if I say "My coffee is hot," we recognize that "coffee" and "hot" are not identical and that the particular coffee I'm referring to happens to be hot now but under different conditions might be cold. The "compositeness" of my utterance (subject verb predicate) matches the "compositeness" of the hot coffee (the coffee is one thing and its temperature another).

When we turn to speak of God, our language will continue to be composite, but this compositeness doesn't suit God the way it suited the composite reality of finite things.[17] So, we need to revise our expectations of what our language is doing when we talk about God, and this is what simplicity is about. Simplicity is a kind of linguistic therapy for God-talk. It pushes us to internalize the mismatch between

16. Burrell, *Aquinas*, 7.
17. Burrell, *Aquinas*, 17.

our language and God. This means that Aquinas's divine simplicity is not a "doctrine of God," because it doesn't purport to *describe* God by stacking up attributes. For Burrell, the entire discussion of simplicity and the following terms like perfection, infinity, immutability, and oneness are ways of shaping our mind to attend rightly to the mismatch between our composite-formed language and God.[18]

Burrell's second strategy, which he develops through comparing the approaches of Aquinas, Avicenna, and Maimonides, finds Aquinas using a distinction from within the creaturely plane to serve as an analogue for "the distinction" between God and creatures.[19] Here he homes in on the importance, pervasive throughout Aquinas's writings, of the real distinction between essence and existence. In Aquinas's Aristotelian metaphysics, the distinction between essence and existence is basic and real for finite beings.[20] Although we can never find bits of "existence" lying around disconnected from "essence" (or vice versa), the two are fundamentally different aspects of all really existing beings. An essence is the definition of a being, that which makes that being the particular kind of being that it is. A human, for instance, is a "rational animal" (a traditional Aristotelian definition). "Rational animal" provides an essential definition of human nature. Existence, by contrast, is the concrete actuality of a being, the *activity* by virtue of which that essence is real and not simply possible. We could express the essence of a unicorn—perhaps very roughly as "one-horned horse"—and yet there are no instances of unicorns outside of fictional worlds. That is, the essence of "unicorn" is only *possible*, it does not actually exist. According to Burrell, this distinction is used by Aquinas to

18. Burrell, *Aquinas*, 16–19.

19. Burrell, *Knowing the Unknowable God*.

20. Aristotle, *Posterior Analytics* 2.7, 92b5–11.

express an analogous difference between God and creature. Because existence is the active power that turns essence from possible to actual, it is analogous to the active power of turning creatures from nonexistent to existent—that is, it is an analogue for God's creative activity. Vis-à-vis creation, God is the active power of unlimited existence, whereas creation (like "essence") has no intrinsic power of its own to bring itself to exist. This strategy uses a real metaphysical distinction that is appropriate to created beings, one that reveals a fundamental compositeness in finite beings, to "show" through our language something of the God who is not composite like this. We can *play* with this metaphysical language—and since this is still a grammatical approach to simplicity, the metaphysical language being used for God is more playful than descriptive—in order to gesture beyond the compositeness of our experience and language to the God who is not rightly conceived in such composite ways. Despite being written as a descriptive, cataphatic statement, "God is simple," is shorthand for the fundamentally negative/apophatic grammatical play we're engaged in when we try to "show" the God who can't quite be spoken.[21]

Burrell exemplifies an approach to divine simplicity that uses "simplicity" as a shaping force in relation to our thinking and speaking rather than as a description of what God is like. While this is not the only way divine simplicity is used in Christian theology, it has had a significant influence, and some theologians who advocate a more metaphysical

---

21. Compare Hinlicky, *Divine Simplicity*. He also develops a grammatical account of simplicity, but his is anti-Thomistic and even attempts a social doctrine of the Trinity with a "weak" form of divine simplicity (by which he means a purely grammatical form of simplicity).

account of divine simplicity still understand it to have a significant grammatical function as well. But is a grammatical account enough? To think through this question, I turn to the "metaphysics of divine being" in the next chapter.

QUESTIONS

1. What is "grammatical" theology? Retell the key historical developments presented in this chapter.
2. David Burrell presents a grammatical interpretation of Aquinas. What is your initial impression of his approach? Can you identify any benefits or drawbacks?
3. This chapter suggests that the grammatical form of simplicity is motivated by the biblical prohibition of idolatry. How significant of a role should the prohibition of idolatry have in the doctrine of God?

3

DESCRIBING THE DIVINE

Simplicity as Metaphysics

And it is an exalted understanding to see and to know inwardly that God, who is our maker, dwells in our soul; and it is a more exalted understanding to see and to know that our soul, which is made, dwells in God's substance; and through this substance—God—we are what we are. And I saw no difference between God and our substance, but as it were, all God, and yet my understanding took it that our substance is in God: that is to say that God is God, and our substance is a creation within God.

—JULIAN OF NORWICH[1]

1. *Revelations*, Short Text, §8.

PART I: THE IDEA OF DIVINE SIMPLICITY

I LIVED IN ENGLAND for about five years. But as someone born and raised in the United States, where we drive on the right-hand side of the road, it took me some time to be comfortable on the roads in England with the opposite flow of traffic. Even after months, there were times I would lose all instincts about the flow of traffic, because I had developed a habit of distrusting my own inclinations. At some point, following traffic in the left lane had begun to feel natural; so when the fact that England and the US follow different rules was brought to my attention, I couldn't remember which inclination to follow and which to distrust. Driving on the right still felt correct, but now so did driving on the left. The negative rule that guided me in the earliest days—something like, "distrust your natural inclination"— became debilitating. Which "natural inclination" should I distrust? This negative rule needed to be overcome with a more positive rule, and I needed to get used to a new inclination that I could trust.

A similar negative rule could be offered as a summary of the view presented in chapter 2, "simplicity as grammar." It would go something like this: *when talking about God, don't trust the normal way language works*. But in this form, do we have any hope of a "new normal" for speaking about God? Or, as happened in my experience with English roads, will this rule inevitably become problematic?[2] This line of questioning captures one concern about apophatic understandings of divine simplicity: namely, that it tends toward agnosticism. This critique doesn't necessarily claim that a grammatical approach to simplicity like Burrell's is agnostic

---

2. See the critique of grammatical Thomism along these lines in Abraham, *Divine Agency*, 1:175–86. Daniel de Haan calls this the "guidance problem" and argues that Aquinas's *triplex via* provides a framework for overcoming it ("Thomist Classical Theism," 101, 109–14).

about the existence of God (as "agnostic" tends to mean). Rather the critique targets the emptiness of our knowledge of God that seems to result from grammatical approaches. With such a strict negative rule about the relation of our language and God, it appears that we really don't know anything about God at all.[3] Practically speaking, this negative rule risks the kind of debilitating lack of confidence I experienced in relation to traffic flowing in one direction or the other. Does divine simplicity only serve to deny the success of our speech about God, or does it also make room for some genuine success? This is part of the issue that a more "metaphysical" approach to divine simplicity intends to address. But this raises the issue of *how* one might relate a metaphysical approach—according to which we do have ways to go on speaking about God—to the grammatical, and what these two are up to.

WHAT IS METAPHYSICS?

Metaphysics is the philosophical task of identifying and ordering the most general, all-encompassing categories by which we understand the world. For this reason, some have called metaphysics the study of "being *qua* being" or the study of being-as-such—not just of one kind of being (like the being of mammals, or the being of natural objects) but of the character and qualities of "being" as borne by all things that exist (often spelled as "Being" with a capital "B").[4] "Being" is arguably the most general category, one in which all real things are included.

---

3. Cf. Gunton, *One, Three and Many*, 23–27, Hinlicky, *Divine Simplicity*, 42–49; and Jenson, *Systematic Theology*, 1:227–29; 2:60–62. For a defense of analogy considering this kind of criticism, see Mascall, *Existence and Analogy*, 104–21.

4. Perl, *Thinking Being*, 1–4.

And yet, many theologians have insisted that God does not belong to the study of metaphysics.[5] Metaphysics can't properly include God because creaturely being and divine being don't fall under one and the same category of "being."[6] Although we say that "God is" or speak of "the divine being" or "God's nature," God's being and creatures' being are radically different "kinds" of being. That is, the word "being" is not univocal (literally meaning "single-voiced"; i.e., having identical, stable meaning) when used of God and of creatures. If "being" isn't univocal, then it is either *equivocal* (meaning that the word is used in completely different, disconnected ways) or it is *analogical* (meaning that the word is used in different but related ways). As the philosopher Barry Miller puts it, equivocity is "casual ambiguity" while analogy is "systematic ambiguity."[7] In other words, equivocity happens when different uses of the same word are arbitrary and unrelated: "cheesy" pasta and a "cheesy" joke have no meaningful connection. In analogy, by contrast, the movement between different meanings is principled or systematic: food is healthy, and a person is healthy; these are related as cause to effect, that is, food is "healthy" to the extent that it contributes to the health of the human body.[8] While most theologians prefer to see some kind of semantic

---

5. E.g., Marion, *God Without Being*, 73–107; but see his careful engagement with Aquinas, concluding that Aquinas's approach can't be called "onto-theology" (199–236).

6. This is one entailment of Aquinas's denial that God is contained in a "genus," which is part of his discussion of God's simplicity (Aquinas, *ST*, 1.3.5). It's also worth noting Aquinas's conviction that God does not fit within metaphysics because metaphysics concerns "common being" (*ens commune*) and God is not a member of common being; see Aquinas, *Commentary on Metaphysics*, prologue.

7. Miller, *Fullness of Being*, 44.

8. Aristotle, *Metaphysics*, 4.2. Book 4 of the *Metaphysics* is often referred to as Gamma (Γ).

connection between uses of the same word for God and for creatures, some have understood the difference to be equivocal or casually ambiguous—we use a word like "good" of creatures and of God, but there is simply nothing in common between the two uses of "good."[9]

If we can follow a "divine grammar" to use words in a systematically ambiguous way (that is, analogically), does this mean that we can directly *describe* God's being? Does analogy allow us to include God as one member—albeit peerless—of a general metaphysics? These are tricky matters. On the one hand, many will want to affirm that our knowledge of God is more than just a knowledge of what God is not, because the latter sounds dangerously like knowing God as nothing. On the other hand, if all our words are used analogically, that doesn't seem to leave a general category working the same for God and creatures that could thereby serve as the basis for a metaphysics in which God is included. Taken together, this rules out a general metaphysics of God and creation and suggests that no matter how much we caution against direct, comprehensive knowledge of God, our metaphysical knowledge and speech surely have *some* connection to God's reality.

GOD AND METAPHYSICS

Let's assume for the moment that our language for God is either univocal or analogical, so some kind of metaphysical language is possible for God. In the sentences "God exists" and "Jonathan exists," the word "exists" *says something* about both God and the author of this book. Minimally it says, "there's at least one of them."[10] But the more meaning

9. E.g., Maimonides, *Guide for the Perplexed*, 1.56.

10. This minimal meaning of "exists" has been treated as the primary meaning of the word in analytic philosophy since Gottlob

"exists" carries, the less obvious it is that the meaning is the same for God and for me. This is called the *analogia entis* ("analogy of being," meaning that even "being" is analogical when used of both God and creatures), and we'll return to that later. So, "exists" might mean the same thing (univocity; e.g., "there is at least one") or something systematically ambiguous (analogy). But what about more ambitious metaphysical work, like the attempt to *describe* something of God's nature, something like "God's nature is love"? Let's apply Augustine's rule, cited in chapter 1: "God is what God has." "God's nature is x" is a possession-claim (God *has* x-nature). But because God *is* what God *has*, the possession-claim needs to be converted to an identity-claim: God *is* x-nature, where x = love. This is an odd sentence, showing how weird divine simplicity can make things. 1 John 4:8 puts it more forcefully: "God is love."

What makes the reformulation so weird is the change from *having* a nature to *being* a nature. This is because "natures" are usually broad categories that include several members. "Jonathan has a human nature" means something like "Jonathan is a member of the category 'human.'" Whatever all humans have in common, be it a shared set of traits or some internal principle of being, it's also enjoyed by me. But this means that I'm not identical to human nature for two reasons. First, because I'm not the only human, and second because I'm not *only* human—i.e., being human doesn't sufficiently describe me. But according to divine simplicity, God is identical to God's nature. And the very same reasons why I'm *not* identical to my (human) nature are the reasons God *is* identical with the divine nature. To

---

Frege. "Existence" is, in this view, merely a quantifier, nothing more (cf. Frege, "Dialogue with Pünjer over Existence"). Consequently, "exists" can be converted from a predicate ("God *has* existence") to a declarative ("There is a God!").

show why this is the case, let's consider how the Christian concept of God works in practice, in particular in the call on all Christians to love God and neighbor. In this way, I suggest that although "God" can't be given a descriptive, "intensional" definition, we can develop an "ostensive" definition—i.e., defining by showing how the word is *used* rather than by listing defining features that must be satisfied.[11]

Christians are called by God to love self, neighbor, and God. In responding to this call (*vocatio*), Christians attempt to discern what is theirs to love and how to love those things in a way that participates in God's love. This means that for Christians, "vocation" is much bigger than a singular calling to a career, but is more like a call to fashion a whole and integrated life.[12] As the philosopher Robert Adams puts it, "vocation is primarily a matter of *what goods are given to us to love*, and thus of *our part in God's all-embracing and perfect love*."[13] The Christian's vocation, then, is to order one's love of the many finite goods immediately present, in discerning attention to how God's "all-embracing" love encompasses each good and oneself. This view of the Christian vocation to love has several elements. First, it has an individual/personal quality: it's about how one's life is dedicated to the cultivation of one's loves in ultimate devotion to God.[14] Second, it has several finite objects: the multiple goods "given to us to love." And third, it has an all-embracing love as its ultimate aim, one that transcends each love while also being intimately present in

11. On "ostensive definition," see Wittgenstein, *Philosophical Investigations*, §28–30.

12. Cf. Hector, *Christianity as a Way*, 175; Coakley, *New Asceticism*, 96–100.

13. Adams, *Finite and Infinite Goods*, 302; emphasis in original.

14. Cf. Hector, *Christianity as a Way*, 174–83.

and to them: ultimately, love and devotion for God (Deut 6:4–5; Mark 12:44). The Christian vocation to love is, in this account, a journey of discernment in which one commits to loving God in neighbor and the neighbor in God (Mark 12:29–31; Luke 10:27).

If this is right, then 1 John 4 provides a powerful account of the internal logic of Christian vocation and some clues to the ostensive definition of God:

> Those who abide in love abide in God, and God abides in them ... We love because he first loved us. Those who say, "I love God," and hate a brother or sister are liars, for those who do not love a brother or sister, whom they have seen, cannot love God, whom they have not seen (4:16b, 19–20).[15]

The implications for vocation are multiple. God's "call" (*vocatio*) to which Christians live in response is the call of love: "We love because he first loved us" (1 John 4:19). Further, because we cannot love the unseen God apart from loving the seen neighbor, it seems that God is only known and loved *insofar as the neighbor is known and loved* ("those who do not love a brother or sister ... *cannot* love God," 4:20; also 2:9–11).[16] Vocation happens where a human love is returned to its source in God. But this response to the "call" of God requires attention throughout one's life to the good of one's neighbors and the good of God given in and through them.

---

15. The Greek here suggests that those who do not love the brother or sister *are not able* to love God (*tòn theòn ... ou dúnatai agapān*), intensifying the sense that love of neighbor is a necessary ingredient in love of God and not merely a *result* of (already) loving God.

16. Cf. Black, "First, Second, and Third John," 431–34; and Yarbrough, *1–3 John*, 263–66; contra Marshall, *Epistles of John*, 225–26. See Lieu's mediating interpretation; *I, II, and III John*, 196–99.

What does this sketch of the Christian vocation to love suggest about the Christian concept of God? First, whatever God is is only knowable through a way of life committed to loving others: "Whoever does not love does not know God, for God is love" (1 John 4:8, interpreted in conjunction with 4:20, quoted above). Second, the one who so loves "abides *in* God," so that they participate in the love-that-God-is (4:7, 16). Third, while God is loved and known *through* loving others, the love of God has a more all-encompassing claim on one's life than does any other love taken by itself (Deut 6:5).[17] Together, this suggests that God stands in a *sui generis* relationship to all things one might love, and that God (and God's nature!) is only known through a particular mode of relating to these things.[18] In this context, God is independent of known concepts or existing defined natures and is a uniquely all-encompassing reality. One knows God by an ongoing, active attention, an attention that is open to every possible (good) object of love. And one must be committed to discerning God in and through all those things.

God, then, encompasses all finite goods, thereby both transcending them (by not being reducible to any one of them and by having a more all-encompassing claim on us) and being fully immanent to them (by being loved only with the love by which we love them). God is not a reality that

17. See also Mark 12:17, where Jesus enjoins his questioners to "give to Caesar the things that are Caesar's and to God the things that are God's." This precedes Jesus's quotation of Deut 6:4–5 in verses 29–30, suggesting that whereas taxes (monetary return) can be claimed by Caesar, it is the whole self ("all your heart . . . soul . . . mind . . . strength") that is owed to God. Then in verse 44, it is the widow's gift of two mites that enacts full devotion, because she gives her whole way of life (*hólon tòn bíon autẽs*).

18. So St. Paul can sum up "the whole law in a single commandment, 'You shall love your neighbor as yourself'" (Gal 5:14), omitting the command to love God and thereby implying that love of God is entailed in right love of neighbor. Cf. Augustine, *Trinity*, 8.10.

satisfies an independently known concept—a descriptive, intensional definition. In fact, the only things we "know" for sure in this account of vocation is that our lives might, through certain practices, participate in God's initiating act of love and that we have a neighbor whom we can see and whom we must love in order to love (and know) God.[19] What appears in this account as a category into which many instances might fall is the *neighbor* whom we see, or as Robert Adams put it in the quotation above, the "finite goods given to us to love" (a phrasing that expands the same logic to include more than other humans). Having a prior nature allowing multiples appears to be a marker of a *finite good*, whereas God is the love by which we love *all* finite goods and in which our love of finite goods finds ultimate fulfillment and direction. God *is* Love, and the way in which God is different from the many local loves is not by the addition of differentiating qualities or properties, but rather by being that which transcends and includes all the local loves with *their* differentiating qualities.[20]

As a term invoked in the context of such a vocational practice, "God" is defined by *use* rather than by straightforward, descriptive *concepts*. Here, "God" names that from which our capacity to love springs and to which our loves ultimately aim. At a more metaphysical level, though, this is a Christian version of the ancient philosophical question of the one and the many.[21] God is the "one" who is known and loved in, through, and beyond the many; the many are

19. Cf. von Balthasar, *Love Alone*, which culminates with his summary statement: "love exists only between persons ... God, who is for us the Wholly-Other, appears only in the place of the other, in the 'sacrament of our brother'" (150).

20. Cf. Nicholas of Cusa, "Learned Ignorance," 1.23; and Spitzer, *New Proofs*, 120–27.

21. The *locus classicus* for this discussion is Plato's *Parmenides*, esp. 132A–B, 132C–133A, 137C–142A, 157B–166C.

known and loved by participation in the one. But this account has already overcome something of the world-evading, body-denigrating character of some Platonic versions of the one-many dynamic.[22] Love of God (and God as love) is not that to which one ascends *in pushing beyond* the multiplicity of the world. Rather, God is known and loved *by participating in* God's active love for the many in the world and so by *direct love of* and *immersion in* the many in the world.

Plainly put, God *is* love, whereas creatures are variegated lovers and beloveds. If God is love (as above, God *is x*-nature, where x = love), then this suggests two things about the relationship between God and the "divine nature." First, as I aimed to show, the relationship is one of identity rather than possession or participation. God doesn't *have* or *share in* "divinity," God simply *is* (and so determines) whatever it means to be "divine," without remainder or additional specification. Second, if God's nature is evoked by a word like *love*, then God's "nature" seems more like an activity than a static, definable "essence" or bundle of properties. As Aquinas puts it, God *is act*.[23] Because the Christian life is a vocation of abiding in the love-that-is-God, we know the *act* of God by *active participation* in that divine act.[24]

Once God's relation to "divine nature" or "divine essence" is converted in these ways, we can draw several implications for the sake of a "metaphysical description" of God as simple. First, a metaphysical description would seek out general categories for God's nature and attribute them to God in a supereminent fashion. God is "love" by inclusively transcending the differentiated "beloveds" in

22. Cf. Plato, *Phaedo*, 95B–E, 108A–C, 114C.

23. Aquinas, *ST*, 1.2.3; 1.3.2.

24. Beautifully explored in Bauerschmidt, *Love That Is God*, 71–91.

the world. What other categories can we attribute to God in this way? The Thomistic tradition has zeroed in on a group of "transcendentals" that might be useful in that way: being, one, true, good, and beautiful. Sometimes, however, the first two, being and one, are seen as implied in the others and consequently redundant, leaving three: true, good, and beautiful. These are called "transcendentals" because they are at once present in each existing thing and in them all things are drawn to ultimate fulfillment and perfection. Because of their inclusive potential, these categories can be used of God, similarly to my use of "love" above. God is not just something good, God is goodness-itself. God is not just something "true," God is truth-itself. God is not just something beautiful, God is beauty-itself. This implies that God is the paradigm of each—e.g., God is the beauty toward which all beautiful things tend and from which all beautiful things receive their beauty. But with these transcendentals, even when saying that God *is* by nature each of them, we still seem to imply that God has multiple grand attributes. In what sense, then, is God metaphysically describable as simple, as having *no parts* whatsoever?

SIMPLICITY AS METAPHYSICAL DESCRIPTION

If truth, goodness, and beauty are metaphysical categories suitable to God for the way they inclusively transcend the many beings that exist, then perhaps they all name a singular reality, just under different aspects. This is, in fact, precisely what simplicity claims. God is the one reality named by beauty, goodness, and truth.[25] In chapter 4, I'll discuss the significance of referring to this as "naming" rather than assigning "attributes" or "properties." For now, the crucial question is: What hope do we have for describing God if

25. Aquinas, *ST*, 1.5.1; 1.6.1–2; 1.11.1; 1.16.5.

these already generalized terms name one and the same reality? Can they name the self-same reality and still retain their distinctive meaning? After all, beauty does not mean the same thing as goodness or truth. Aquinas suggests this isn't a severe problem, because of the way these terms apply to God—namely, by way of God's activity as the creative source of all beautiful, good, and true things. They apply to God somewhat "indirectly." This means they could be related to a more fundamental descriptive term without being invalidated. And Aquinas knows of such a term: being. I said above that "being" (along with "one," in some accounts) doesn't need to be listed as one of the transcendentals because it's implied by them. That's because "being" is the more fundamental reality of which truth, goodness, and beauty are corollaries. Consequently, God can be described by the term for that more fundamental reality—God is being-itself, in Latin: *ipsum esse subsistens* or just *ipsum esse*.[26]

Aquinas has two reasons for prioritizing this metaphysical description for God, and they are motivated by Christian convictions rather than mere philosophical reasoning. First, Aquinas believes this description is an interpretation of Exod 3:14, God's provision of a "name" to Moses: "I AM WHO I AM . . . Thus shall you say to the Israelites, 'I AM has sent me to you.'"[27] God provides this name to Moses, and it seems to identify God directly with the verb "to be" ("I AM" or "THE ONE WHO IS"). Second, Aquinas understands God's revealed identity as creator to provide warrant for describing God as *ipsum esse*. In simplest terms, to call God creator is to claim that God is the one who gives

---

26. Aquinas, *ST*, 1.4.2. Aquinas uses *ipsum esse* as a shorthand for *ipsum esse [per se] subsistens*. The inclusion of "*subsistens*" conveys the self-subsisting sense in which God is "being-itself."

27. See the discussion of this verse at the end of chapter 4.

existence to that which would otherwise not exist. But God can only *give* existence if God has a uniquely strong relationship to existence. In fact, if God can give existence, then either "existence" is some kind of reality alongside God that God can use or mold to make things, or existence is somehow strictly *internal* to God. The former way of speaking has generally been viewed as incoherent or mythological. The latter then remains; if existence is internal to God, then either God divides up something inside God in order to create (sending out parcels of divine-being-as-existence in order to bring creatures into existence) or God *is* existence in a more intimate and radical sense.

Aquinas opts for this final choice and, in the process, transforms the concept of "existence" and its metaphysical status.[28] To capture the unique flavor of Aquinas's concept of "existence," interpreters often prefer to keep his concept in untranslated Latin: *esse*. *Esse*, which I introduced above in the description of God as *ipsum esse*, has for Aquinas a richer meaning than "existence" evokes in modern use. *Esse* is not merely a way of quantifying, a way to say "there's at least one of these things"; rather, *esse* is an active principle, a power to stand forth from nonbeing.[29] According to Aquinas, to exist at all is to be *in act*.[30] And the internal dynamic power of *esse* is that it is the deepest act by which being communicates or reveals itself.[31] There are two aspects to the act of existence (*esse*) in creatures: to exist is (1) to have been *given* existence and (2) to have the power to actively shape existence, both through self-determination and by affecting others. God's act of existence is analogous but not

28. Gilson, *God and Philosophy*, 63–73; Clarke, *Explorations in Metaphysics*, 5–15, 45–52, 79–82.

29. Clarke, *Explorations in Metaphysics*, 6–8, 12–15.

30. Cf. Clarke, *Explorations in Metaphysics*, esp. chs. 1, 3, and 10.

31. Clarke, *Explorations in Metaphysics*, 8–10.

identical. God's *esse* is that which (1) is an unlimited, unbounded act of existence and (2) does not shape or reshape itself but can *give* existence by self-donation.

God *is* (by nature) God's own, infinite act of existence—*ipsum esse subsistens*. Because God's relationship to the divine nature is one of identity rather than possession, God is identical to this infinite act of existence. Two further metaphysical claims follow: God is pure act (*actus purus*) and in God existence and essence are identical. First, God is pure act. This means that God is "act" or "actuality" without mixture of "potentiality." Potentiality has two aspects, "passive potentiality" and "active potentiality," and the relation to "pure act" is different for each. Passive potentiality means "a way something could be but presently is not" (a modification or change to an already existing thing). Active potentiality means "the power to do something." For example, I may want to become a competitive cyclist. In that case I have the "passive potentiality" of "being a competitive cyclist" (since it's a hypothetical possibility for me to have that trait, but it's not currently the case), and I have "active potentiality" to the extent that I already have the basic ability to ride a bike, an ability I would need to actively employ in training for competition. God's "pure actuality" entails a total absence of passive potentiality. That's because pure actuality signifies an entirely fulfilled and complete act of being, and for such a plentiful reality, "modification" has no meaning (how do you modify that which is *the* active, dynamic source of every possibility of modification?). But as pure act, God does have "active potentiality" (the power to do or make happen).[32] Pure actuality, though, transcends the distinction between actuality and active potentiality: God is not a mixture of being-in-act plus an unused or hypothetical power to act more. God's pure being-in-act

32. Cf. Duby, *Divine Simplicity*, 81.

simply is God's power to act.[33] So, for God the pure actuality of existence is identical to the active potentiality to do something. Thomas Weinandy reflects on this through the lens of love and passion:

> If there were changeable and passible passions within God, as these are found in human beings, it would mean that he is not fully loving for he would have to actualize further "loving" potential.... God is supremely passionate because he is supremely loving and he is both because both are fully in act since God as *ipsum esse* is pure act.... God is impassible precisely because he is supremely passionate and cannot become any more passionate.[34]

God cannot become more active—whether in terms of love or passion or creative self-donation—not because of a lack in God (as "cannot" might seem to imply) but because God is already entirely active without any reserve. "God is light and in him there is no darkness at all" (1 John 1:5). Because God withholds nothing from God's action, God's action is the pure actuality of *esse* unrestrained (and so unconditioned by passive potentiality). God is *actus purus*.

Second, in God existence and essence are identical. In ordinary usage, existence and essence point to different features of beings: the essence of something answers to the "what is it" question and the existence of something answers to the "is it real/actual" question. We can imagine many kinds of things that *might* exist (a unicorn) or *could* exist (a new fastest breed of horse) without claiming that they in fact *do* exist. In other words, essence does not entail existence, or "what" something is doesn't entail "that" it is. Similarly, that something exists does not fully determine "what"

33. Cf. Davison, *Participation in God*, 165–67.
34. Weinandy, *Does God Suffer?*, 126–27.

it is, because the identity of beings is formed through time and through their actions and interactions. So in creatures, essence and existence are distinct, even if inseparable. This is called the "real distinction." But is this distinction real in God's case? The answer issues from the above discussions. If God is God's nature, and that nature is "being itself," and this "being itself" is *actus purus*, then God's "nature" or "essence" simply is God's existence. In other words, where essence and existence are two poles of creaturely being (poles needed for the dynamic development of creaturely being through time and relations), in God these are not "poles" but are entirely transcended in their difference (or, as Kathryn Tanner formulates it, non-contrastively transcended).[35] God's active, abundant reality is more inclusive and whole than what appears in creatures as the "real distinction." And we can invoke this more fundamental, transcendent mode of being by saying that what in creatures are distinct (essence and existence) are identical in God's case.

So a "real distinction" in creatures (between essence and existence) provides a way to mark "*the* distinction" between God and creation. As David Bentley Hart says, "Both one's essence and one's existence come from elsewhere . . . and one receives them both not as possessions secured within some absolute state of being but as evanescent gifts only briefly grasped within the ontological indigence of becoming."[36] God, by contrast, is the giver, the self-diffusive activity underlying the interplay of essence and existence characteristic of creaturely becoming. The essence-existence identity can be expressed in a few different ways. We could say, for instance, that what makes God God is not the *possession* of an essence that distinguishes God's kind from other kinds; rather God is distinctly God by being nothing

35. Tanner, *God and Creation*, 37–48.
36. Hart, *Experience of God*, 92.

other than the act of existence.[37] God is distinctly God by having no need of a distinctive "quiddity." This is a metaphysical way of saying what in chapter 1 was discussed as "persisting in asking unanswerable questions." We ask the question of God's essence/nature/quiddity in order to clarify the specific way in which God's quiddity can't be defined. Or we could just say, again, God is *ipsum esse subsistens*.

This discussion has already delivered a hefty set of metaphysical claims about God: God is identical to God's nature, God is *ipsum esse*, God is *actus purus*, and God's existence and essence are identical. There are then several additional metaphysical claims that follow, which can be noted briefly now, but some of which will receive further discussion throughout the rest of the book. With the above claims put forward, we can also conclude that God is absolute, particularly in the sense that God has a distinctly singular reality that is self-sufficient, underived (*a se*, hence "divine aseity"), eternal, omnipotent, and immutable.[38] Second, God is "necessary," but in a particular sense; most fundamentally God is "necessary" as the source and ground of all being, first God's own (as *ipsum esse*) and then secondarily as the ground of created being.[39] And finally, all attributes or properties that we might attribute to God are identical in God's being.[40] That is, although we use a lot of different words to describe God's character and nature (words like "wise," "good," "faithful," "everlasting," "merciful," "jealous," etc.), these words do not refer to different

---

37. "The [*esse*] which is God is of such a kind that no addition can be made to it, whence through its purity [this *esse*] is distinct from every other [*esse*]" (Aquinas, *On Being and Essence*, C5, §90).

38. Dolezal, *God Without Parts*, 67; Stump, *Aquinas*, 92–130.

39. Cf. Schärtl, "Einfachheit und Trinität," 397–406.

40. Aquinas, *ST*, 1.3.6; Duby, *Divine Simplicity*, 85–86; Dolezal, *God Without Parts*, 125–63.

properties or different traits in God's reality, since God's reality is not divisible into parts. This is one of the most controversial aspects of divine simplicity, and theologians and philosophers of religion have put forward radically divergent interpretations.[41] Some of the controversy, however, revolves around disagreement about how language for God works. For this reason, we'll return to this topic in the next chapter with the discussion of "divine names."

METAPHYSICS AND THE (GRAMMAR OF?) DIVINE DIFFERENCE

Already we can see that a "metaphysical" form of simplicity will acknowledge that it names God's being differently than the same language would name creaturely beings. We can also conclude that knowledge of God as simple (again, if "simple" means something more than just grammar) is not directly deducible from our experience and knowledge of creatures, at least not without some kind of transformed vision through the revelation of God as creator. Beyond these two points, there's another reason that a metaphysical construal of simplicity needs a partner in the grammatical construal—viz., "simple" is *not a divine property or attribute at all.* This would hold for two reasons: first to turn "simple" into a property would be incompatible with the way metaphysical categories had to be transformed and stretched in using them for God. For instance, understanding *actus purus* required the admission that God's being-as-act *transcends* the difference between act and potency. So an attempt

---

41. For a representative sampling of critics, see Plantinga, *Does God*, 46–61; Radde-Gallwitz, *Basil, Gregory, and Divine Simplicity*, throughout, but for summary see 5–9; and Wolterstorff, "Divine Simplicity." For a sampling of defenses, see Brower, "Divine Simplicity"; Mann, "Divine Simplicity"; Stump and Kretzmann, "Absolute Simplicity"; Vallicella, "Divine Simplicity."

to employ a contrastive term like "simple" (determined by contrast with "composite") as a univocally descriptive property would be to reify an abstract, relative concept as though it were an element of God. Fittingly, the grammatical function of simplicity disallows treating anything as a straightforward property of God, precisely because that approach problematizes the composite structures of our language in respect of God, who is not amenable to such compositeness. Second, "simple" is not a property because that would be internally inconsistent, claiming that God is not composite and then attributing a composite relation between the subject (God) and the property ("simple").[42]

To say that divine simplicity is "metaphysical" is to say that it is about more than just pointing out the limits of our language. It's not merely grammar—even if it is at least grammar. Following Burrell, I said that grammatical simplicity is a way to rework our language to *show* something about God that can't be *said*. If simplicity is *more* than this grammar, as this chapter has been exploring, then we have two options for trying to reconcile metaphysics and grammar, reintroducing the distinction between "univocity" and "analogy" from above. Either simplicity (1) says something *directly* of God (univocity) and grammar is a secondary consequence, or (2) simplicity underlies *judgments* about God's *sui generis* reality, enabling metaphysical description only through systematic modulation of our language (analogy). I'll call the first approach "univocal metaphysics" and the second "analogical metaphysics."

Univocal metaphysics would heavily qualify and subordinate the grammatical approach and use simplicity to make direct descriptive attributions to God. Even if "simple" is not a property, this approach would treat other attributions as "real" in God. Here one might conclude

---

42. Aquinas, *ST*, 1.3.3, 1.3.6.

that the grammatical account is simply overstated, making more fuss than is reasonable from the Creator–creature distinction.[43] By contrast, this approach might start with some or all of the central metaphysical claims associated with divine simplicity—that God is the First Cause, is infinite, perfect, immutable, eternal, etc.—and then consider what (if any) grammatical implications emerge for other God-talk.[44] In this univocal approach, we might say that divine simplicity is a metaphysically descriptive claim about God that, because of its core shared meaning with other simple realities (like subatomic particles), gives us a clear sense of how some of our language has to be adjusted to work for God, but doesn't make the more radical claim that *all* of our language needs (apophatic) reworking.[45] For instance, claiming that God is metaphysically simple would disqualify all language of change, logically entailing immutability. Something that is simple simply can't change, because all change implies movement of parts, some kind of addition or loss of parts, or modification of form. Something that is absolutely, metaphysically simple has no parts or distinct form that could undergo modification, therefore whatever is absolutely simple is also immutable (incapable of change). This would require us to grammatically qualify all narratives or descriptions of God that seem to imply change ("God *became* man"), but this view would do so on the basis of a univocal attribution of "immutability" to God. So, it would appear that we "know" what kind of unchangeableness

---

43. E.g., Abraham, *Divine Agency*, 1:175–86.

44. Again Abraham, *Divine Agency*, 3:62–3, for whom simplicity is only appropriate to express a minimal sense of indivisible unity. He develops his critique of the metaphysics of divine simplicity further in 4:30–6.

45. E.g., Crisp, "Parsimonious Model of Simplicity," 558–73.

obtains for God, and as a result we "know" how to convert apparent change-attributions into changeless ones.

The difficulty with this approach to a metaphysical view of divine simplicity is that it tends to speak of the divine essence as if it is its own metaphysical entity, which, for the doctrine of the Trinity, would threaten to become a fourth reality in relation to the three divine persons. And, further, what the grammatical account of simplicity captures powerfully—the radical difference between God and creation—seems downplayed or left as an afterthought. When this difference is downplayed, we risk taking too much for granted about our capacity to recognize and express God's reality, and at worst we risk a kind of conceptual idolatry by too readily identifying God with finite, creaturely modes of being or conceptualization.

Analogical metaphysics takes a different approach, synthesizing the grammatical and the metaphysical more thoroughly and less *post hoc*. A fuller account of analogical metaphysics will emerge in chapter 4 with an account of analogy and participation. But here we can explore it at a more schematic level in two ways: Aquinas's *triplex via* and Hildegard of Bingen's mystical theology. Aquinas formalizes the integral role of analogy in theological metaphysics through his *triplex via*, meaning "threefold way."[46] In this account, we must perform three operations on our claims in order to both test them and transform them for proper use of God. Aquinas puts it this way:

> We know of God's relationship with creatures: [1] that He is the cause of them all; [2] also that creatures differ from Him, inasmuch as He is not any of the things caused by Him; [3] and that such is denied of Him not by reason of any

46. Aquinas, *ST*, 1.12.12. For analysis, see De Haan, "Thomist Classical Theism."

defect on His part, but because He superexceeds them all.[47]

The three steps on the way to right speech about God are: (1) affirm something of God by virtue of the Creator–creature relation, then (2) deny anything that is only a creaturely aspect, and finally (3) rework it to express the supereminence of God. Theologians as early as Philo of Alexandria (c. 20 BCE–40 CE) and, after him, Gregory of Nyssa (c. 335–95 CE), sensed something like this pattern in Moses's life: (1) Moses pursued the light of God in the burning bush (Exod 3), (2) he entered into divine darkness (Exod 20:21), and (3) he desired to behold God's glory (Exod 33).[48]

So, we can and ought to call God "good" (step one), not least because in creating, God affirms that all that's made is "good . . . very good" (Gen 1:4, 31), and the goodness of creation is purely a gift of the God who alone is good (Mark 10:18). But (step two) God is "not good" in the way creatures are, for the latter's goodness is ephemeral, contingent, and easily obscured or rejected (1 Chr 5:11–26; Ps 16:1–4; Gal 6:1–10). But this "not good" has nothing to do with a lack on God's part, whether a qualitative or quantitative lack or a lack of the dynamic mutuality of goodness-in-relationship. Rather (step three) the "not good" is subsumed under the ever-greater goodness of God that transcends competition, gradation, and contingency (Pss 16:1–2; 23:5–6; 100:5; 119:64–8; Matt 7:11; Rom 5; Jas 1:17). God is simply Goodness-itself. This *triplex via* both integrates grammar with metaphysics and articulates a way to overcome the debilitating potential of a purely negative grammatical rule.

---

47. Aquinas, *ST*, 1.12.12 (alt.).
48. Cf. Soskice, *Naming God*, 124–25.

PART I: THE IDEA OF DIVINE SIMPLICITY

Second, Hildegard of Bingen demonstrates a more mystical-interpersonal context for knowledge of God (as simple), and in this context an "I–Thou" form of address transforms all metaphysical talk.[49] Our knowledge of God emerges first in the second-person mode of address to the God who is the object of our prayer, and then it is inflected by our attempt to direct others to a second-person encounter with this reality. This shift to the second-person accomplishes two things: first it locates speech about God within the Father–Son relationship, so that we speak about God by virtue of participating in God. Second, it specifies the content of that speech because the sense of particular attributions we might make of God have their first home in the filial (Father-Son) relation by which we have second-person knowledge of God.

Hildegard writes about God from the perspective of union with Christ, which places her work within an "I–Thou" vantage point—again, speaking "about" God from a primarily second-person position of sharing in the filial relation between Father and Son.[50] So, for instance, in order to "discover" whether paternity is distinct from God, Hildegard trains her attention, "look[ing] carefully *to the true Light* . . . for we human beings are not capable of learning about God in the same way that we learn about the humanity of other human beings."[51] This gives context to one of the

49. For an account of how theological claims are re-framed through the shift to an "I–Thou" posture, see Knauer, *Glaube Kommt Vom Hören*, esp. 198–203. Similarly, McFarland, "God, the Father Almighty," 264–67.

50. Hildegard of Bingen, *Scivias*, 2.2. In this vision, Hildegard sees the human figure of Jesus in a face-to-face encounter, with the Father like an "exceeding bright light bath[ing] the whole" and the Spirit as a "lambent fire that suffused the whole human figure, so that the three existed as one light in one power of potential" (alt.; PL 197:449A).

51. "Letter to Odo of Soissons," in Hildegard, *Selected Writings*, 22.

striking features of Hildegard's theological writing, which is the way she shifts from God's first-person perspective to the human first-person perspective, sometimes without signaling the change.[52] To speak of God is to constantly re-express one's self in relation to God, finding one's own vision of the "true light" only through being held within the vibrant gaze of this light itself. Such contemplation of God cultivates a confidence in the transcendent substantiality of God as the one in whom the praying subject's true being is located. In this way, Hildegard presents us with a judgment about God as the ultimate substance—*a se*, uncaused, utterly transcendent, and perfect—but this judgment is not an ordinary descriptive claim in the third-person mode. Rather, the judgment is formed by the moment of prayer and confession. It is in surrendering the self to God as one to whom the self is addressed, in whom the "I" lives and moves and has its being (Acts 17:28), that one recognizes God as the singular sufficient "substance": as perfectly "simple."[53]

Hildegard invokes divine simplicity in a way that self-consciously unites the regulative and metaphysical functions. This demonstrates the possibility of bringing them together in a way that takes seriously the kind of depth grammar advocated by Burrell, without demoting theological language to a merely regulative function. Both Hildegard's contemplative approach and Aquinas's *triplex via* provide ways to integrate grammar and metaphysics. Aquinas enables a kind of third-person description of God that overcomes some risks of unqualified apophaticism. Hildegard invokes a more doxological approach that involves the speaker in personal address to God, so that the "descriptive" power of human language for God is grounded in a

52. E.g., Hildegard, *Book of Divine Works*, 1.1, 1.3.
53. Hildegard of Bingen, *Selected Writings*, 21–22.

second-person encounter with God's reality. Hildegard's approach sets the debilitating risk of grammatical simplicity in the context of worship, providing a solution tailored to that domain. With these possibilities at hand, we can turn directly to the question of how we address and name (the simple) God.

QUESTIONS

1. What's the difference between univocity, equivocity, and analogy?
2. This chapter argued that the word "God" has an ostensive definition within the Christian vocation to love, and that this enables metaphysical claims about God. Is that enough to warrant the kind of metaphysics explored in this chapter?
3. Which approach to analogical metaphysics do you prefer: the *triplex via* of Aquinas or the Hildegard-inspired interpersonal reframing? How would you articulate the benefits of one over the other?

4

BEING AND NAMING

Simplicity, Scripture, and Language for God

> O fresh viridity of God's creative finger,
> in which God planted a green vineyard
> that glistens in the heights, a lofty pillar:
> You are glorious in the preparation of God.
> —HILDEGARD OF BINGEN[1]

NAMES PLAY A VITAL role in personal relationships. They bind us together, conveying individual uniqueness and connectedness. V. E. Schwab, in her novel *The Invisible Life*

---

1. "O viriditas digiti Dei" (alt.). The phrase "fresh viridity" translates Hildegard's coined Latin term "viriditas," which means "greening power" and is used by Hildegard as a name for God, especially for the Holy Spirit.

PART I: THE IDEA OF DIVINE SIMPLICITY

of Addie LaRue, explores the deep power of names. Out of a desperate hope to escape a poorly matched wedding, the eponymous character, Addie, sells her soul for complete freedom from relational obligations. This "freedom" is granted in the form of tracelessness: she leaves no marks, no memories. She can live forever and cannot be claimed by anyone else. She learns, though, that this also means she can't be *named*, not really. She's incapable of writing or speaking her given name, and so she is also incapable of being addressed by name. The implication is that to be named is to be claimed, to have connections, to leave marks—and that lacking these things isn't really *freedom*.

Throughout Scripture naming is a powerful action. The first human (*ha 'adam*) names all the other animals, realizing in the process that none would make a suitable partner (Gen 2:19–20). Later, after the human pair is sent out of the garden, the male partner, Adam, asserts his now sin-deformed power by naming the woman "Eve." In this act, Adam sets Eve in a subservient role, treating her like one of the "unsuitable" animals in Genesis 2 and binding her to function as "mother of all living" (Gen 3:20).[2] If giving a name imposes a power-relationship, what hope did Israel have for referring to God by name? Without a divine name, how could Israel articulate its claim by God? Although Israel can't name God, God provides a name (Exod 3:13–16). Israel is not able to name God, for that would be a kind of subordination of God. And yet, God provides a name out of a desire for intimacy.[3] This name is an act of self-revelation; no wonder, then, that Israel treats God's name as holy (Pss 99:3, 105:3–5; Isa 57:15). The holiness of God's name is professed out of the conviction that no human thoughts—and, by implication, no human words—are

2. Trible, *Rhetoric of Sexuality*, 133–35.
3. Fretheim, *Exodus*, 65.

adequate for addressing or describing God (Isa 55:8–9; Job 38:1–40:2; and in the NT: John 1:18; 1 Tim 6:16).

This gives God's name a unique status in Scripture. God's name is just as much a token of God's *ineffability* as it is of God's *intimacy* and *accessibility*. Although God's name doesn't permit anyone to manipulate God—as though uttering God's name would put God under the speaker's control—God does "dwell" by virtue of the divine name. The position of God's name in Deuteronomy, for instance, is associated with God's presence and promise (e.g., Deut 12:5, 11, 21). The Lord places the divine name as a sign to Israel of where the Lord is leading them, the place where they shall dwell and worship: "You shall seek the place that the Lord your God will choose out of all your tribes as his habitation to put his name there. You shall go there" (Deut 12:5). Only God can bring about such dynamic, personal dwelling in the divine name, so eventually in Jewish practice they resist pronouncing the divine name altogether.[4] In the biblical world, names not only point to the one named, but they also bear something of the reality of the one named.[5] Jordan Barrett refers to this rich connection between God's name and God's presence as "the hypostatic character of the divine name," articulating a strong sense of the ontological weight and particularity of the divine name—a weight and particularity that is nothing other than the "weight" of divine glory itself.[6]

The person who first names God in Scripture is Hagar (Gen 16:1–14), and her act of naming provides an important paradigm for how divine naming works in Israel's life and, I think, for theology in general. While Adam's act of naming Eve was also an act of Adam coercively *determining*

4. Soskice, *Naming God*, 20.
5. Bohmbach, "Names and Naming," 33.
6. Barrett, *Divine Simplicity*, 148, also 137–55.

Eve's future (you will be mother of all living!), Hagar's act is commentary on God's *self*-disclosure.[7] Hagar finds herself in the wilderness, having been "dealt harshly with" by the jealous Sarai (16:6), and in this alienated state, God hears her and sees her (16:7–12). In response to God's address, Hagar names God, saying, "You are El-roi, by which she meant, 'have I not gone on seeing after He saw me?'" (16:13, NJPS).[8] Calling God "El-roi," meaning "God of seeing" or "God who sees," echoes God's naming Hagar's son "Ishmael," meaning "God hears" (16:11). Her name for God, then, is not a way of binding God to a future role; rather, it is a response to God's self-revealing action. God actively *hears* and *sees* Hagar, and by way of praising God for this action, Hagar names God El-roi. Phyllis Trible concludes, "Hagar is a theologian. Her naming unites the divine and human encounter: the God who sees and the God who is seen."[9] In a sense, to be a theologian at all—to be one who speaks of God—is to follow in Hagar's steps, and so to follow Hagar's example of praising God by name.

DIVINE SIMPLICITY AND THE DIVINE NAME(S)

The theologian's vocation is to attest to God's self-disclosure by praising God's name and praising God through names. Not only is this appropriate to divine simplicity as I've

---

7. A similar contrast could be made between Sarai and Hagar in the narrative of Gen 16. Phyllis Trible says, "For Sarai, Hagar is an instrument, not a person" (*Texts of Terror*, 11). Like Adam's domineering act of naming, Sarai attempts to possess and determine Hagar's future by making Hagar a surrogate for Sarai's own future desires (cf. Williams, *Sisters in the Wilderness*, 4–5, 15–31). Hagar's encounter with God and naming of God suggest a different, liberatory kind of relationship.

8. Cf. Trible, *Texts of Terror*, 18, for translation notes.

9. Trible, *Texts of Terror*, 18.

presented it so far, but it's one way in which divine simplicity's construal of God's nature might be *more* compatible with Scripture than are those approaches that catalog divine "attributes" or "properties."[10] Here is the place to return to that contentious element of the metaphysics of simplicity from the previous chapter, namely that God is identical to all divine "properties" and so all divine "properties" are identical to each other—the so-called "identity thesis." For many theologians and philosophers, this is the final nail in the coffin for divine simplicity. The identity thesis appears to run into insurmountable problems, either reducing all our language for God to empty synonyms or reducing God to a mere property or an "abstract object." Nicholas Wolterstorff raises the first concern, arguing that if in God wisdom and goodness are identical, then the sentences "God is wise" and "God is good" *mean* the same thing, which would be problematic.[11] Alvin Plantinga articulates the latter concern, arguing that if God is identical to God's properties so that all God's properties are identical, then God is *nothing other than* a "property," which is an abstract object and not a concrete, personal reality.[12] Both criticisms miss the mark, because they both conflate the mode of speech with the reality spoken of (the *modus significandi* and the *res significata*).[13] The synonymy critique assumes that where there is identity at the level of being (ontology), there must be identity at the level of linguistic meaning (semantics). However, the names "morning star" and "evening star" refer to one reality (Venus) without being synonyms, since the names are relative to the positions of the earth and sun when Venus is visible. And the abstract object critique

10. See Soskice, *Naming God*, 9–39.
11. Wolterstorff, "Divine Simplicity."
12. Plantinga, *Does God*, 57.
13. Aquinas, *ST*, 1.13.4.

assumes that by identifying God's being with words that in some contexts denote "abstract objects," one reduces *God* to such an abstract object.

But more fundamentally, both criticisms assume that when we say something about God's nature, being, or character, we're attributing a *property* to God corresponding to a *component* of a descriptive definition. This assumption itself is a modern development, and one that deserves some scrutiny.[14] Through the philosophical writings of René Descartes (1596–1650) and John Locke (1632–1704), theological epistemology radically shifts. Epistemology in general becomes an obsession with the "trauma of not knowing."[15] In his post-Cartesian context, Locke tries to figure out how we can "know" God. Locke rejects the earlier notion that humans are born with "innate ideas," the idea of God among them. And in his struggle to find an alternative basis, he reframes the idea of God. In fact, for Locke the *idea* of God is primary, because he believes we can only claim to "know" God if we have a descriptive definition of "God" and can match this idea to an objective reality. This then assigns a distinctive role to the qualities we associate with God—as constituents of the definition of God, they are components of right knowledge of God.[16] This stands in stark contrast to the discussion in chapter 3, where I rooted the concept of God in practices, in "ostensive" rather than "intensional" definition (the latter of which Locke assumes). Locke deploys a *philosophical* assumption that forces a particular *theological* construal of God's being. That is, the components of the definition of God are only "true" (and sufficient for knowledge) if they correspond to really distinct "properties" or attributes in God.

14. My account here is inspired by Soskice, "Naming God," 241–54.
15. Soskice, "Naming God," 242.
16. Locke, *Essay Concerning Human Understanding*, 1.4.

The divine names tradition evokes a radically different conceptuality. Thinking of God's characteristics through the lens of "names" assumes the pattern established by Hagar—that to speak of God is to attest to God's self-disclosure in concrete, messy history. It depends, then, on two theological convictions: that God acts in self-communicative ways and that God is the creator of all. Taken together, this means that something of God's own character and fullness is refracted throughout the diversity of creaturely realities. Pseudo-Dionysius the Areopagite (likely between the late fifth and early sixth centuries) develops one of the earliest Christian philosophical approaches to divine names. His is a synthesis of Christian theology, spiritual exegesis, and neo-platonic philosophy (especially influenced by Proclus). Because he wrote under the name of one of those converted through St. Paul's preaching at the Areopagus (Acts 17:34), many in the medieval church granted his texts near apostolic authority.[17]

In Brendan Sammons's study of Dionysius's understanding of divine names, he puts forward this definition: "As used by Dionysius, a 'divine name' identifies a perfection of God that proceeds from his superessential plenitude into the intelligible order manifesting itself through various existential phenomena."[18] In other words, a divine name is God's fullness on display in and through the finite, material elements of creation (Rom 1:20). Sammon draws out the implication that "divine names constitute a degree of porosity between the symbolic and the ineffable, the material and the spiritual."[19] Naming God relies on the conviction that the transcendent God is pervasively present in the immanent plane of creation, suffusing and thereby transfiguring

17. Louth, *Denys*, 111–29; Sammon, *God Who Is Beauty*, 89–90.
18. Sammon, *God Who Is Beauty*, 113.
19. Sammon, *God Who Is Beauty*, 116.

creation into words of praise to God (Ps 65). We can address God, "not by giving him names but by using the names that he has revealed."[20] Divine names are drawn from created particulars, used for God in worshipful response to divine self-disclosure, and addressed to God in all-transcendent plenitude. If this sounds reminiscent of Aquinas's *triplex via* (ch. 3 above), that's no accident, given the significance of Dionysius's influence on Aquinas.[21] The crucial result, which highlights the contrast between divine names and divine "attributes" or "properties," is that a divine name is addressed to the *entirety* of God, rather than only a part. Dionysius says,

> All the names appropriate to God are praised regarding the whole, entire, full, and complete divinity rather than any part of it, and that they all refer indivisibly, absolutely, unreservedly, and totally to God in his entirety.[22]

Divine names do not represent *parts* of God that satisfy the semantic content of the word in its ordinary usage. Rather, divine names praise *the whole* of God as the generous source and immanent presence that proceeds in and through the creaturely domain and is manifest within creation under the aspect of each name. Dionysius's approach powerfully contrasts with the "divine attributes" tradition and makes significant progress in overcoming the apparent problems of the "identity thesis." The divine names are *not* identical to each other, because they are named of God from a particular creaturely vantage point (how God's creative procession is manifest within a concrete creaturely domain), but *what*

20. Louth, *Denys*, 78.

21. Dionysius the Areopagite, *Divine Names*, 2.1 640B–C. On Dionysius's influence on Aquinas's *triplex via*, see O'Rourke, *Pseudo-Dionysius*, esp. 31–41.

22. Dionysius the Areopagite, *Divine Names*, 2.1 636C.

they name is simply the one, self-same, undivided fullness of God. "And so it is that as Cause of all and as transcending all, he is rightly nameless and yet has the names of everything that is."[23]

Roughly a century later, St. Maximus the Confessor (580–662 CE) discusses similar matters, and he uses explicitly christological reasoning to justify a kind of affirmative, cataphatic speech about God (embedded nonetheless in a robust apophaticism).[24] Commenting on Jesus's transfiguration (Matt 17:4–8; Mark 9:6–8; Luke 9:28–36), Maximus suggests that the transfiguration displays both God's unknowability and God's revelation through creatures.

> The light from the face of the Lord, therefore, conquers the human blessedness of the apostles by a hidden apophatic theology. According to this [light], the blessed and holy Godhead is by essence beyond ineffability and unknowability and countlessly raised above all infinity, leaving not the slightest trace of comprehension to those who are after it.[25]

Concerning the "affirmative mode of theology," Maximus suggests that Jesus's transfiguration leads us to see all created things as "radiant garments of the Lord" by which we encounter God's activity as the creator and fashioner of all. Maximus uses a highly developed notion of the intrinsic logic or nature of each thing—its "logos," to use the Greek term—to consider how creatures might become transfigured, radiant garments revealing their creator. That each creature has a "logos" (a nature or intrinsic logic) becomes

23. Dionysius the Areopagite, *Divine Names*, 1.7 596C.

24. For an account of how Maximus's Christo-logic transforms categories of participation and goes beyond Dionysius, see Wood, *Whole Mystery of Christ*, 63–83.

25. Maximus the Confessor, "Difficulty 10," 1168A.

a way to relate each to Jesus and therefore to God, since in John's Gospel Jesus is revealed to be *the* Logos of God (John 1:1), through whom all things are made (John 1:3; Col 1:15–17).

This suggests that knowing God is not simply a matter of knowing what God is not, as if to know God only as nothing. Rather, through the light of Christ (John 1:4, 9), God's own generous love is made visible in the goodness and logic of God's creatures. The saints in particular, Maximus says,

> gaze intently on the highest attributes (*logoi*) concerning God that are accessible to men, by which I mean his goodness and his love, from which they learn that God is moved to give to what exists being and to grant to them wellbeing . . . by the grace of the great gift of God, they have become manifest images of the radiant, ineffable and evident glory.[26]

Through meditating on God's goodness and love, saints are brought to see God's generosity and creativity more fully and may then become "manifest images" of God's glory. Consequently, the saint is able to see that "In [God] the *logoi* of all good things, as in an ever-bubbling spring, preexist in accordance with the one, simple and unique embracing of all things, and they draw to him all those who use well and naturally the powers given them for this purpose."[27] Created things can be radiant garments of God displaying the transfiguring glory of Christ, the Word by which they are spoken, because God is the "simple and unique" preexistence of all created *logoi* (Eph 2:10; Col 1:17).

---

26. Maximus the Confessor, "Difficulty 10," 1204D.
27. Maximus the Confessor, "Difficulty 10," 1205C.

So far, we've seen that with the twin affirmations of (1) God as simple creator and (2) Jesus as the Word (*Logos*) of God through whom all creatures have their intelligible being (*logoi*), we can move toward contemplation of God's being by way of intimacy with creatures (Ps 104:24–33). Further, an affirmation of God's simplicity functions to relate the diverse, manifold *logoi* to their perfect convergence in God. But as Ian McFarland puts it, "Considered by themselves, the *logoi* of creatures are like words of a novel taken out of context, the significance of which cannot be understood apart from some prior grasp of the one divine Logos who is their source and end."[28] So, even if we can contemplate God through creatures, apart from divine illumination—particularly the revelation of Christ—we will not be able to understand directly the God who is creation's source and end. This qualification fits with Maximus's use of the transfiguration as the event that teaches the disciples to see all creaturely *logoi* as "radiant garments of the Lord." Our intellectual and contemplative powers are enabled by grace to know God through the mirror of creation (1 Cor 13:12). This confirms from a different direction that "metaphysics" is not one self-contained study including God and creation, because for our knowledge of God to relate to our knowledge of creatures, God must draw our attention to God in a way that would not happen through our study of creatures alone. The path from creatures to God, at least in terms of knowing God's being and character, is not direct or automatic. And so, although divine names derive "from creation," they aren't fully understood without Christ's action and transfiguring presence.

28. McFarland, *From Nothing*, 81–82.

PART I: THE IDEA OF DIVINE SIMPLICITY

SIMPLICITY, ANALOGY, AND PARTICIPATION

St. Maximus provides a christological concentration for a Dionysian approach to the divine names. Beginning with Dionysius's understanding of names as God's plenitude proceeding in and through the variety of creaturely goods, Maximus helps to concentrate this into a statement of the Son's procession as the all-encompassing *Logos* by which the individual *logoi* receive their character and to whom they all point. Naming the entirety of God through multiple names is a doxological response to the revealing and transfiguring work of Christ.[29] This raises questions about how creation relates to God and how language spans the interval between God and creation. The former is the question of participation, the latter analogy.

In chapter 2, we saw that Burrell suggests that the real distinction between existence and essence is an analogy for the unbounded existence of God as the creative source of creaturely being. In this context, "simplicity" might do more than govern our language and might also express a judgment with metaphysical significance (ch. 3). The judgment expressed is that God exists and exists as Creator of all else—all else being brought into existence by the action of God. If existence is that by virtue of which each kind of being is made actual, then by analogy, God is the principal act by which all else is made actual. God is the active power of existence without bounds, overflowing to share existence with creatures (which would not have existence otherwise).[30] Simplicity is, then, *both* (1) an apophatic control on our language, formalizing a grammar of divine difference, *and* (2) a judgment about the unlimited creative

---

29. Barth, *CD*, II/1, 326.

30. Which qualifies Burrell's strictly grammatical approach; cf. te Velde, *Aquinas on God*, 73–77.

activity of God, the plenitude of God's life, and the non-contrastive transcendence of God.[31]

By shifting to divine names, I'm suggesting that simplicity regulates our language in an "analogical" way (not merely as a generic denial of our linguistic potential in respect of God), and thereby cultivates specific judgments about God. As one interpreter characterizes Aquinas on analogy, "Analogy is usage based on judgment."[32] A judgment is an "act of comparison and reflection in the process of coming to know the truth."[33] That is, a judgment is an intellectual act by which we discern the appropriateness of speaking about or conceptualizing reality in a specific way. In making a judgment, we are actively moving from perception and experience to understanding and appropriate expression. In relation to divine simplicity, I've been arguing that simplicity is a grammar for proper talk about God *and* that it expresses a judgment about God's unique reality. Divine simplicity does not *describe God* directly but rather expresses a *judgment about God's difference from creation as a function of God's unlimited creative activity and incarnational-transfiguring activity*.

Simplicity tells us that when we think of God (and speak of God and know God) this is in a radically different mode than the way we think (and speak of and know) creatures. But rather than leave us with an empty "unknown" on the divine side of that difference, simplicity is also instrumental in analogically spanning the difference—that is,

31. The possibility of such an interplay eludes Barry Smith in his *Oneness and Simplicity*, 114–19. He writes as if a proper apophaticism is constrained to literal negations when speaking of God, whereas the interplay of analogy and apophaticism in Thomism, and in traditions strongly influenced by him, see negation as always involved in a form of affirmation (the *triplex via*).

32. Rocca, *Speaking the Incomprehensible God*, 158.

33. Rocca, *Speaking the Incomprehensible God*, 164.

simplicity is useful in providing guidance for the systematic ambiguity needed to reflect on the difference well.[34] So what is analogy? Let's explore two ways to interpret Aristotle's *pros hen* analogy, where food, a human body, and urine can each be called "healthy." First, John Duns Scotus (c. 1265–1308) argued that even analogical use of language often depends on a deeper underlying univocal meaning (crucially, in the case of "being" used of God and of creatures), so that in the end his metaphysical account of divine infinity and simplicity is a kind of "univocal metaphysics."[35] Food, a human body, and urine can each be "healthy," but the meaning of health is not identical in each case. Aristotle's analogy suggests that food and urine can be rightly called "healthy" because of the way they are related to the human body, which is the proper site of health or unhealth. Food is healthy if it is productive of bodily well-being, and urine is healthy if it is produced by (and so provides evidence of) a healthy body. In Duns Scotus's view, although the three uses differ, there is a univocal conceptual core connecting them, something like, "pertaining to bodily well-being." They each "pertain to bodily well-being" differently, but the three uses of the word share this same core meaning.[36]

For Aquinas, by contrast, this is an example of analogy and *not* univocity. One "meaning" or semantic core is not identically repeated in the three uses. At the merely linguistic level, they differ so much that it appears *equivocal*. However, the use of "healthy" across the three instances can

---

34. So Peter Leithart's suggestion that "composite" could be analogically predicated of God (Leithart, "What Sorts of Parts") rests on a misunderstanding of the distinction between analogy and equivocity.

35. Though this is a contested matter amongst interpreters of Duns Scotus; cf. Ashworth and D'Ettore, "Medieval Theories of Analogy," §7.

36. Duns Scotus, *Questions on Aristotle's Categories*, 2.19.

be systematically coordinated by virtue of the way food and urine are related to bodies. The appropriateness of using "healthy" for food and urine hinges on our ability to make a judgment about how they are related to bodily health at the level of being, but not because there is a univocal core at the linguistic level. The body is the "primary analogate"—the thing properly called healthy—whereas food and urine are "secondary analogates"—only called healthy by relation to the body. If the use of words for God is analogous in this way, then we can see how it would affect our understanding of a word used of both God and creatures. If we say, for instance, that God is "good" and that a tree is "good" and that an action is "good," then we are making judgments about the relations between these things rather than claiming there is one identical feature that obtains for all of them. Further, according to the *pros hen* analogy, the judgment consists of seeing the goodness of a tree or an action as consisting in a particular relation to the prime good, God. For key terms—especially the transcendentals: beauty, goodness, and truth—thinking analogically means seeing God as the primary analogate. Consequently, fully understanding the goodness or beauty or truth of any created reality requires a judgment about its relation to God, like understanding healthy food and healthy urine requires a judgment about how healthy food causes the health of a human body and healthy urine gives evidence of it.

In the example of food, Aquinas's interpretation suggests that relations at the level of being make the analogical use of words possible. In the case of God and creation, *participation* at the level of being makes analogical speech for God possible.[37] Because God is the creator, the one from whom all creaturely reality flows, God is the "primary analogate." However, several things about that relationship

37. Davison, *Participation in God*, 173–76.

are different than the body, food, urine analogy. God is the true and full "good," like the human body is the true locus of "health." But creatures are not means by which God is made "good" (in the way food produces health in the body). To that extent, the analogy fails. However, we could think of the human body as the "final cause" of the "health" of food; that is, food is healthy insofar as its health-producing-potential is "realized" in a human body. A metaphysics of participation suggests something similar between God and the creature: God is the *final cause* (or telos) of creatures' goodness, so that the potential for goodness in creatures is realized to the extent that the creature is fulfilled through intimacy with God.[38] In the case of urine, it was "healthy" to the extent that it provided *evidence* of the health of a human body. This is possible when one knows the causal relationship between the human body and its urine. Creatures do not really "give evidence" of the qualities God has, since we do not have the requisite understanding of the "causal" relationship between creator and creation. But the mystery of God's goodness is indirectly manifest in the finite goodness of individual creatures. Although we do not directly know the proportion or the mode of creation's exemplification of divine perfections, all that creatures are and have are refracted gifts of that which is full and complete in God.[39] We can then speak of God's "goodness" indirectly as the paradigmatic goodness for all created goods.

Put together—that God is the paradigmatic "good" and the telos of creaturely goods—this suggests a specific relationship between creatures and God. God does not dispense goods into an "outside" realm; rather, creatures have their goods *by participation*, a direct sharing in the perfection that God is (Rom 11:36). This suggests that the relation

38. Davison, *Participation in God*, 113–31.
39. Oakes, *Pattern of Redemption*, 25–44.

between God and creation is one of thorough intimacy, mediated only by the "analogical interval"—the *manner* in which a creature exemplifies (in a partial, refracted, and particular way) what is full, replete, and simple in God.[40] As David Bentley Hart puts it,

> The event of the world simply is the occurrence of this analogical interval, the space in which beings rise up from nothingness into the light that gives them existence.... The *analogia entis* (in its developed form) does not concern a grasp of being at all; rather it introduces an analogical interval into being itself, because it has already grasped that the God Who Is is nonetheless no being among beings.... Thus theology can imagine an analogy between an *esse* that is participated in by what subsists, without diminution or constriction, and a transcendent act of being that is also subsistence: the life of God. Being itself is different in God, because God is not a being, yet is; he does not belong to being, but is being, and yet subsists.[41]

An "analogical interval" at the level of being (*analogia entis*) is a difference (between God and creatures) that is otherwise than all other differences (between creatures). Therefore, the analogical interval takes place as the embrace of all created being by the fullness of God's own being. As Edward Oakes (1948–2013) summarizes, "A theory of analogy [is] not to grasp at God but to explain why God cannot *be* grasped! Not to claim God but to explain why God can, and does, claim us!"[42] This captures the significance of

---

40. Dionysius, *Divine Names*, 1.3 589C; Nicholas of Cusa, "Learned Ignorance," 1.6, 1.16–18, 2.2.
41. Hart, *Beauty of the Infinite*, 131, 232, 233.
42. Oakes, *Pattern of Redemption*, 43.

analogical language and the *analogia entis* within the divine names tradition. In addressing God by name, we can't define God's being or bind God to a subservient role, but rather address God according to God's self-revelation and the claim God makes on our creaturely life.

EXODUS 3:14: THE ONE WHO IS

Scripture celebrates God through many names. Hagar names God "El-roi," the God who sees. Divine names are not properties that enable some picture-like description of God's metaphysical make-up. Such an account is problematic, because God's unique reality transcends the subject-predicate distinction and because God proceeds forth in and through the many creaturely realities according to which God is manifest (Ps 104). This suggests, as Dionysius reasons, that God can be named with an infinite variety of names—as varied and numerous as the variegated beauty of creatures.[43] Many of these names, perhaps most, are pure metaphor—names like "Rock" (2 Sam 22:2–3), "Light/Star" (Rev 22:5, 16), life-giving "Dew" (Is 18:4, Hos 14:5), etc. Dionysius even grants elevated status to the most overtly metaphorical names, like "Worm" (connecting Ps 22:6 with Christ) because of the extreme mismatch: "so that those with a real wish to see the sacred imagery may not dwell on the types as true."[44] But one name at least seems more than metaphor, YHWH—the name God provided to Moses from the burning bush (Exod 3:15–16) and is presented as "the LORD" in English translation.[45] Some consider this name to be a play on the Hebrew verb *hayah* ("to be"), which would then echo God's declaration in 3:14, *'ehyeh 'ašer 'ehyeh*,

43. Dionysius, *Divine Names*, 1.6–8 596A–597C.

44. Dionysius, *Celestial Hierarchy*, 2.5 145A.

45. Soulen, *Divine Name(s)*, 7–14.

translated as "I AM THE ONE WHO IS" or "I WILL BE WHO I WILL BE."[46] It was a common-place throughout medieval and scholastic theology to connect "I AM THE ONE WHO IS" with the metaphysical claim that God is *ipsum esse*, being-itself. This connection now reeks of the worst of scholastic prooftexting.[47]

Reimagining this connection, however, might serve both to tie together elements from this chapter's discussion of divine names and to reorient the significance of Exod 3:14 for divine simplicity beyond prooftexting. I suggest that this text orients Moses (and the reader) to God's indescribable identity in a way that grounds trust in the radical uniqueness and incomprehensibility of God's reality. Divine simplicity—especially under the aspect of *ipsum esse*—explicates this radical uniqueness and incomprehensibility. But if Exod 3:14 is to be reconnected with *ipsum esse*, it will be necessary to recall the meaning of *ipsum esse* established in chapter 3. "Being-itself" is not a direct *description* of God's "being" as a maximal instantiation of some static "stuff"; rather, calling God "being-itself" is an expression of the divine surplus of activity/actuality that transcends any delimiting distinctions and boundaries. It expresses the unlimited, infinite act of "existence" that God is and by virtue of which God is the creator of everything else.

God's self-declaration that "I AM THE ONE WHO IS" is first an act of divine self-gift—God is present, addressing Moses through the fiery bush and, in the future relative to

46. Because of the ambiguity, I alternate between the translation options. Whether this permits any "metaphysical" interpretation is a contested, though still relevant, question. Cf. Childs, *Book of Exodus*, 75–77; Moberly, *Old Testament*, 81; and Saner, *Too Much to Grasp*, 109–29, 202–3.

47. Adler, "What's in a Name?," 265–69; Smith, *Oneness and Simplicity*, 59–60; but see the generous and comprehensive treatment of Moberly, *Old Testament*, 61–67, 69–86.

the text, leading Israel to freedom. Second, this self-ascription is given in the mode of promise—proceeding forth into the future and evading any static temporal reference. God's utterance comes in response to Moses's request for a name by which he might gain the trust of the Israelites (3:13). But more fundamentally, Moses seems to be asking for a "name of power," a name that authorizes his mission and that will prove to Israel (and Pharaoh) that Moses is acting by God's initiative.[48] God responds by evading a typical name, and so God seems to bypass the request for a simple token or handle by which Moses could invoke God's action and authority. But it's not obvious that God denies Moses's request altogether, for God does recommend that Moses say to the Israelites, "I AM has sent me to you" (3:14b). Despite the oddity of this "name," it is still part of God's direct response to Moses's request. And at the same time, it's supplanted in the following verse when God gives the Tetragrammaton (YHWH) and says, "*This* is my name forever, and *this* my title for all generations" (3:15). Consequently, "I AM THE ONE WHO IS" is not *the* divine name, but it is *a* divine name. Through the future/imperfect tense, it roots God's future saving action purely in God's active power ("I WILL BE WHO I WILL BE"), and so it is a "procession of God's plenitude" in and through a creaturely event (the liberation of Israel).

By rooting God's future action in God's active power, this name provides a complicated response to Moses's request. At one level, God grants the request, telling Moses what to say to skeptical Israelites. But at another level, God roots Moses's action, his commission, in God's own reality.

---

48. God and Moses's previous discussion (3:1–12) suggests that this exchange is not merely about confirming to Israel that Moses was sent by their God (that could have been demonstrated by the earlier introduction God offers in 3:6). Rather Moses seeks a name by which *he* will make things happen. See Saner, *Too Much to Grasp*, 121–22; and LaCocque, "Revelation of Revelations," 311.

Moses must respond with trust to THE ONE WHO IS/WILL BE, and, in and through Moses's faithful obedience, God performs the promised liberating action. As with Hagar, this "naming unites the divine and human encounter."[49] "THE ONE WHO IS" becomes a name for God as an embodied way to celebrate the fullness of God's self-revealing action manifest in the liberating work commissioned through Moses.[50] God's plenitude can't be reduced to some static "metaphysical-ontological" perfection—"Being," attributed univocally. Rather, the name resists *any* reduction of God's being, for God exceeds the labels or handles by which Moses might seek to deploy divine power. Consequently, it's unhelpful to root God's identity in the future (a univocal "WILL BE") in such a way that God's actions become the *means* by which God self-determines, because doing so construes God's actions as at least partly selfish—God acts in creation in order to become this kind of God rather than that, and God would then use creaturely events to achieve God's identity. Rather, God's "I AM/WILL BE" is a word of promise, which, as Brendan Sammon puts it, "posits the plenitude of divine being as the overfullness of determinacy."[51] The "overfullness of determinacy" of the "name"—the way the name remains both ambiguous and irreducible—suggests that the fullness of God's "to be" is *knowable* through human participation in God's action, rather than "determined" through such action. And though this does not directly denote *ipsum esse*, it makes a comparable judgment about the unbounded plenitude of God that exceeds any "name of power" and can only be known through active involvement.

This name serves to bind God's people and God's representatives to God's very self. It also enables second-person

49. Trible, *Texts of Terror*, 18.
50. Cf. Cone, *God of the Oppressed*, 57–66.
51. Sammon, *God Who Is Beauty*, 101.

address and in so doing reciprocally joins God to God's people and, in this case, to Moses.⁵² The "being" of Moses is drawn into God's own "being" by the mysteriously capacious utterance, "THE ONE WHO IS"—a name that exceeds the "IS" in holding forth the promissory "WILL BE."⁵³ In this way, Moses's encounter with "THE ONE WHO IS" in 3:14 is further intensified when God allows the divine glory to pass by him (Exod 33:13–34:9), because there, too, God's glory is a proceeding-forth, commissioning a corresponding movement of faithfulness in Moses. And so Moses is drawn into a mystery that he must perform and continue to address by name, but also a mystery that is simultaneously *beyond* the grasp of every performance and *fully present* in the act: the simple, infinite being of God—THE ONE WHO IS, or *ipsum esse*.⁵⁴

QUESTIONS

1. Can you articulate the difference between the "divine names" tradition and the "divine attributes" tradition? What do you make of this distinction and its implications?

2. What is the significance of "participation" and the "analogy of being"? What connection do these concepts have with divine simplicity?

3. The chapter ended with a meditation on "I am the One who is." How well does this connect divine simplicity with Exod 3:14?

---

52. Similarly, Barth, *CD*, II/2, 342–43.
53. Soskice, *Naming God*, 32, 126–29, 212–16.
54. See also Platter, "Simplicity and Scripture," 295–306.

PART II
EXPERIMENTS IN CHRISTIAN DOCTRINE

The goal of Part I was to explore the meaning of divine simplicity and how it affects God-talk. Let's take stock. Simplicity is a way of persisting in asking the unanswerable question, "What is God?" This requires us to invoke a particular grammar for God-talk, a way of consistently remembering the mismatch between our ordinary ways of speaking and the unique reality of God. But a merely grammatical approach seems doomed to undercut our ability to go on talking about God, so some kind of "metaphysical" or descriptive approach seems necessary. This produces some complicated and hefty claims like God is *ipsum esse* (being-itself), God is *actus purus* (pure act), and that God's existence and essence are identical. Making proper sense of these claims requires holding the grammatical and the metaphysical together (analogical metaphysics), which means employing something like Aquinas's *triplex via* and/or, like Hildegard, reorienting to a second-person mode of address. Following these possibilities leads to a divine names approach to theological language: in speaking "about" God, we are actually "naming" God in doxological response to God's self-revelation. Speaking "about" God is like Moses's (eventual and sporadic) act of faith, living into the "I AM/WILL BE" of God's self-gift in liberating promise. Now in Part II, the question is: how does this account of God's simplicity bear on key doctrines? Can it be integrated consistently in articulations of God's triunity (ch. 5), the act of creation (ch. 6), incarnation (ch. 7), and the substance of Christian hope (ch. 8)?

5

TRINITY

These three Persons exist as one God in one integral, majestic divinity: and the unity of the divinity lives inseparable in these three Persons, because divinity cannot be rent apart, since it always remains inviolable, altogether without changeability.

—HILDEGARD OF BINGEN[1]

GOD IS THE MYSTERY of infinite actuality, unbounded existence in eternal self-donation. To speak in this way is to utter a partially formed truth, the power of which (as currently expressed) lies in its apophatic character. To articulate more adequately the eternal self-donation of the divine life—and so also to specify "infinite actuality" and "unbounded existence"—requires overtly trinitarian language. This is so for two interrelated reasons: first, the statement's apophatic character means that it simultaneously

1. Hildegard, *Scivias*, 2.2 (my translation; PL 197:449).

says more and less than is adequate to God's eternal life. Second, Christian articulations of God revolve around the mystery of the Holy Trinity, so that a doctrinal account of "what" or "who" God is involves explicit reflection on the revealed relations of Father, Son, and Spirit. Echoing my invocation of Evelyn Underhill in the Introduction, Katherine Sonderegger frames the doctrine of the Trinity this way, "This is the intellectual dignity of the Mystery of the Holy Trinity, that It sends forth Its Consummate Reality to the ends of the earth, even . . . the question and thirst for Reality Itself. The search for the real is the trace of the Trinity in human endeavor."[2]

There are two important theological questions for integrating divine simplicity and Trinity. First, there is the vexed dichotomy between two "treatises" in the doctrine of God: *De Deo Uno* (on the one God) and *De Deo Trino* (on the triune God), a dichotomy Karl Rahner (1904–1984) famously criticized, both for its excessively "Western" flavor (à la the so-called "de Régnon thesis") and for its complicity in a practical "mere monotheism" in Christian piety.[3] These are matters of "trinitarian architectonics." Second, there is the (logical) question of whether simplicity and Trinity can be integrated coherently—i.e., doesn't "three persons" necessary entail some kind of complexity or composition, in which case it would contradict divine simplicity?

In light of these concerns, theologians in the trinitarian revival often oppose a "properly trinitarian" theology to ones associated with simplicity. Christoph Schwöbel (1955–2021) expresses the opposition cleverly in his summary of the influence of Barth and Rahner: "The answer to the question about the identity of God is for Christian faith,

2. Sonderegger, *Systematic Theology*, 2:197.
3. Rahner, *Trinity*, 10–21.

therefore, a triplicity and not a simplicity."[4] In this chapter, I address Rahner's concerns summarized above and the challenge that Trinity and simplicity are contradictory. In the process, I argue that the heart of the impasse may lie in the terms of Schwöbel's summary, in particular the notion that simplicity or Trinity purport to be *the answer* to the question of the identity of God. To that end, I return to the discussion from chapter 3 on the meaning of "God" in the context of the Christian vocation to love. Through dialogue with St. Augustine's interpretation of 1 John 4, I argue that we should understand "Trinity" (and simplicity) through the lens of *practices that sustain our questions* about the identity of God rather than as a straightforwardly descriptive *answer* to such questions.

TRINITARIAN ARCHITECTONICS

A major concern of the trinitarian revival has been the structure of doctrines of the Trinity, "trinitarian architectonics." If we say God is *one* being in *three* persons, is it right to start with an account of the one being or the three persons? The so-called "de Régnon thesis" uses this lens to distinguish between "Eastern" and "Western" approaches to the Trinity.[5] Named after Theodore de Régnon (1831–1893), the "de Régnon thesis" diagnoses problems within Western (Latin) theologies of the Trinity by contrast with Eastern (Greek) theologies. The principal issue concerns the Western preference for starting with the oneness of God. Colin Gunton (1941–2003) summarizes,

---

4. Schwöbel, "Trinitätslehre als Rahmentheorie," 33 (my translation).

5. It is "so-called" because it is not an accurate characterization of de Régnon's own conclusions. Cf. Barnes, "De Régnon Reconsidered," 51–79; and Butner, "For and Against de Régnon," 400–408.

> The real difference [between the East and West] tends to be . . . in the way in which the oneness and threeness of God are weighted in relation to one another, and whether, as often happens in the West, the oneness outweighs the threeness and makes the persons functionally indistinguishable to all intents and purposes.[6]

If Gunton is right, beginning with the divine essence and affirming a strong form of simplicity have led the West to a minimalist—or worse, an inconsequential—articulation of the three divine persons in their particularity. Gunton and others compare select analogies for the Trinity as support for their assessment. One of Augustine's favored analogies is a single (simple) mind and the three faculties of memory, understanding, and will (or love).[7] This is called the "psychological analogy." Gregory of Nyssa, by contrast, offers a "social analogy," starting with three persons, Peter, James, and John, and arguing for a strong sense of the unity between persons where they are engaged in joint action.[8]

On the surface, these two analogies illustrate Rahner and Gunton's distinction perfectly, and simplicity is a serious culprit. In Augustine's analogy, God is like a single human mind with three faculties, in which case, the three are not "persons" in any meaningful sense, they are not *inter*personal, and they are so entangled as to produce actions of a single acting subject, at least as seen from the outside of that mind. Consequently, the "persons [are] functionally indistinguishable," reducing to a singular "simple" substance without robust personal distinctions.[9]

---

6. Gunton, "Eastern and Western Trinities," 43–44.

7. Augustine, *Trinity*, 10.4.

8. Gregory of Nyssa, "Not Three Gods" (*NPNF*2 5:331–36).

9. Gunton, "Eastern and Western Trinities," 44; see also Jenson, *Systematic Theology*, 1:110–14.

Trinity

By contrast, Gregory's analogy affirms three robustly distinct persons (just like three human persons), the unity of which appears to emerge from their joint activity.[10] In these terms, Gregory's analogy is far superior for understanding persons (divine and human) as incommunicable and particular. Gregory's use of person-language seems to enable a strong sense of particularity-in-community (as seen in the Trinity's unity through joint activity), and consequently Gregory's view seems perfectly suited to overcoming modern Western hyper-individualism. The fact that simplicity is more obviously connected to Augustine's psychological Trinity is all the worse for simplicity. Gregory's superior trinitarian theology seems to construe God's unity in social terms, and so God's "oneness" is interpersonally composite and therefore *not* simple.

Although I am sympathetic with the egalitarian and non-individualistic goals that are often associated the perspective I've just sketched, the trinitarian arguments remain problematic in several ways, particularly because the opposition between Augustine and Gregory has been exaggerated.[11] The differences in analogies are not indicative of differences in substance, for three reasons: first, the analogies are context specific. Augustine was responding to the *homoians* who rejected Nicaea's "same nature" (*homoousios*) in favor of a "like" nature (*homoiousios*), and Gregory to another person's question of how three "persons" wouldn't result in three gods. These differences mean that their analogies are tailored to emphasize a specific side of a dilemma. Second, they are both apophatic thinkers and attentive to the severe limits of their analogies. And third,

10. Plantinga, "Social Analogy"; and Plantinga, "Social Trinity and Tritheism."

11. Barnes, "De Régnon Reconsidered," 51–79; Coakley, "'Social' Trinity," 117–24.

PART II: EXPERIMENTS IN CHRISTIAN DOCTRINE

several key moves in their treatments match each other in substance, especially their shared conviction that the unity of operation *ad extra* expresses a singular power *essentially*. This final point is crucial for appreciating the lack of a "social" doctrine of the Trinity in Gregory of Nyssa. He doesn't argue that the *unity of God* is produced by the persons' joint action, but rather that the *unity of action* is produced by a singular power and therefore singular "being."[12]

If Augustine and Gregory are not as opposed as it at first seems, much of the impetus for obsessing over "trinitarian architectonics" is undercut. But Rahner's ultimate concern wasn't primarily the *ordering* of the "one" and the "three"; he was more concerned about a practical "mere monotheism" that made the Trinity a speculation about the eternal life of God (the "immanent Trinity") with no bearing on human life in history (the "economic Trinity," meaning the Trinity in the work of salvation). For Rahner's adherents, simplicity played a key role in driving a wedge between the immanent Trinity and economic Trinity. Simplicity intensified the unity of God's acts *ad extra* ("to the outside"), so that how God acts in relation to creation seems to be a function of the undifferentiated "essence" rather than particular divine persons. But God's revelatory activity is meant to draw creatures into relationship with God's very self; if God's eternal life is cut off from our life in history, then what we encounter in Scripture and history is not a genuine *revelation* of God for the sake of communion, because God's eternal life remains inaccessible and distant, hidden *behind* "revelation." To address this problem,

---

12. Gregory of Nyssa, "Not Three Gods" (*NPNF*2 5:334–35). Consider also Gregory of Nazianzus's "Oration," 31.16 (also called the Fifth Theological Oration): "each of the Trinity is in entire unity . . . by identity of being and power," in Gregory of Nazianzus, *On God and Christ* (*NPNF*2 7:323). See Anatolios, *Retrieving Nicaea*, 218–20.

Rahner offers an axiom, now known as Rahner's Rule: "The 'economic' Trinity is the 'immanent' Trinity and the 'immanent' Trinity is the 'economic' Trinity."[13] That is, God's eternal life as Trinity is identical to God's life as Trinity in salvation history, and vice-versa.

This axiom elegantly and compellingly attests to the genuine presence of God (immanent Trinity) in God's saving revelation to us (economic Trinity). Many of its interpreters rightly sense that this axiom doesn't work well with divine simplicity, at least if taken to certain extremes. And at the same time, it is deeply ambiguous. How is it that God's triune revelation and triune eternity are identical? In the wake of Rahner's initial formulation, there seem to have been three major options:

1. **The immanent Trinity *drives* the economic Trinity.** Developed by David Coffey and often associated with T. F. Torrance, this construal argues that the first part of Rahner's Rule works at the level of our *knowledge*: we learn about the Trinity first through the economy (giving *epistemological* priority to the economic Trinity). The second part of the Rule works at the level of God's *being*—the revelation of the Trinity is an expression of who God is in eternity (giving *ontological* priority to the immanent Trinity).[14] Because the immanent Trinity has ontological priority, the unity of the immanent and the economic derives from the *eternal* (immanent) triunity of God. In this version, a modest understanding of divine simplicity might have a role, if it supports the kind of distinction between the persons revealed in the works of salvation and

---

13. Rahner, *Trinity*, 22.

14. Coffey, *Deus Trinitas*, 13–27; Torrance, *Doctrine of God*, 6–7, 30–49.

avoids reducing all God's actions to functions of an undifferentiated divine essence.[15]

2. **The economy *is* the Trinity (period).** In her masterpiece, *God for Us*, Catherine Mowry Lacugna prioritizes the first part of Rahner's Rule, arguing that the economy is the proper domain of trinitarian doctrine. The idea of an "immanent Trinity" is something like a category mistake, an attempt to peer into the mystery of *theologia* (the eternal, incomprehensible reality of God).[16] Christian teaching on the Trinity is nothing other than practical and spiritual reflection on the Christian life as participation in the Spirit's and Son's missions by which we are brought into fellowship to the Father. This too permits a form of divine simplicity, apophatically construed, if it doesn't detract from the trinitarian shape of the Christian life.

3. **The economic Trinity *will be* the immanent Trinity.** The "theologians of hope" (e.g., Jürgen Moltmann, Robert Jenson, and Eberhard Jüngel) argue, in their own ways, for a "futurist ontology," in which God's "eternal" being is defined eschatologically. To speak of an "immanent Trinity" independently of created history is to invoke a myth, one that depends on a "Hellenistic" prejudice that the realm of "becoming" (changeable things under the conditions of time) is a passive and deceptive shadow of real "being." This is a "protological" construal of God's being, and it inevitably reduces the vicissitudes of history to the mere unfolding of what is already foreknown and predetermined in God's actualized being. By contrast, the theologians of hope argue that the biblical God doesn't

---

15. Cf. Torrance, *Doctrine of God*, 173–74, 194–202.
16. Lacugna, *God for Us*, 223.

work from the past *pushing* things into being but from the future *calling* things into the eschatological kingdom. God's eternal, "immanent" being as Trinity is also a future reality, ultimately what God *will be* as history's "becoming" comes to fruition.[17] This view is often the most critical of divine simplicity for the way that ideas like *actus purus* seem to articulate an "achieved" actuality (in eternity *past*) that is opposed to change, passion, and development.[18]

These are distinctive positions, all claiming roots in Rahner's Rule. And the extent to which each approach is compatible with simplicity varies. The worthy aims of Rahner's Rule turn out to be ambiguous in its implementation. Rahner's Rule aims to affirm the unity of God's life, undivided between eternity and time. However, it centers talk of *two* Trinities to such an extent that it's difficult to avoid the impression of an irreducible binary requiring coordination.

Despite my reservation about the ultimate value of Rahner's Rule, each variation has important lessons for any attempt to articulate the Trinity. The first view helpfully frames the relationship between epistemology and ontology; its lesson is that the order of thinking ought to be grounded as cohesively as possible in an account of God's unique, eternal reality (L1). The second emphasizes the practical, lived, and embodied dimension of trinitarian thought; its lesson is that the doctrine of the Trinity is not primarily a matter of directly describing God's eternal being but marks a "who" question sustained in practices by

17. Moltmann, *Trinity and the Kingdom*, 10–20, 129–78; Jenson, *Triune Identity*, 1–10, 57–61, 103–14; and Jenson, *Systematic Theology*, 1:63–114; Jüngel, *God's Being*; and *God as Mystery*, 184–225, 368–96.

18. But see my argument that something of the grammar of divine simplicity is still at play in Jenson's theology: Platter, *Divine Simplicity*, 104–35.

which we participate in the triune movements of God in creation (L2). The third view raises the question of whether affirming pure actuality ends up removing God from the history in which God is revealed as Trinity and, with that, ends up disempowering creatures as purely passive effects of God's pretemporal determination; the lessons here are that God isn't known through abstract identification with one temporal pole but through attention to the concrete details of the New Testament (L3), and creaturely being must have its own integrity and power to act (L4). Lesson 4 (L4) will most adequately be incorporated in the chapters on creation and incarnation.

Fig. 5.1—Lessons from the Variations of Rahner's Rule		
L1	Keep the order of thinking about the Trinity grounded in the eternal life of the Trinity.	Imminent *Drives* the Economic
L2	Keep practices of participation in the triune activity of God at the center.	Economic *is* the Trinity (period)
L3	Don't reduce God to one temporal pole but identify the Trinity through attention to the NT.	Economic *will be* the Immanent
L4	Don't neglect the integrity and activity of creatures when affirming God's eternal actuality as Trinity.	

ASKING (AGAIN) UNANSWERABLE QUESTIONS

These explorations in "trinitarian architectonics" raise several issues for the connection between divine simplicity and the Trinity: discussing the "de Régnon thesis" prods us not to allow a starting point or an analogy to over-determine the doctrine of the Trinity.[19] For divine simplicity, it raises a

---

19. As Sonderegger says, "The deep things of God cannot be had through intellectual architectonic; we cannot rearrange the bits on the theologian's desk so that all works out neatly and well" (*Systematic Theology*, 2:51).

serious question about how such a thoroughgoing account of God's "unity" can be sustained without diminishing the eternal relationality of Father, Son, and Spirit. Additionally, some attempt to integrate the lessons from the three variations of Rahner's Rule will be necessary. I suggest that two moves can be made which resituate trinitarian doctrine and divine simplicity in requisite ways. First, I return to my initial framing of simplicity as *persisting in asking unanswerable questions*, so that the Trinity could be thought of in a similar way (integrating L2 and L3). Second, I return to the divine names tradition to consider how trinitarian naming is analogous to the general kind of naming presented by Dionysius, though trinitarian naming uniquely expresses God's *internal* processional life (integrating L1) *as well as* the way God's perfections proceed forth in and through creaturely realities (further integrating L2).

So: how is the doctrine of the Trinity a way of persisting in asking unanswerable questions? Rather than the "what" question, the Trinity has its proper home in the "who" question: *Quis sit Deus?*[20] This is still a question about knowledge, and one, as St. Augustine noted, inflected by affective concerns.[21] We should love God, but how can we love God without knowing who God is?[22] Following the lead of 1 John 4:7, "because love is from God; everyone who loves is born of God and knows God" (and conversely, in v. 8, whoever doesn't love doesn't know God), Augustine sees the activity of loving as itself the matrix for knowledge of

20. Aquinas, *ST*, 1.32.2: "in God essence signifies a 'what' [*quid*], whereas person signifies a 'who' [*quis*]" (my translation).

21. The question "who are you?" doesn't always require a descriptive answer (i.e., "My name is so-and-so, I'm the child of so-and-so," etc.). The question can be an expression of wonder: "who *are* you?!" (like Inigo Montoya's question to the masked Westley in *The Princess Bride*), a form of the question to which the appropriate response is further interaction.

22. Augustine, *Trinity*, 8.6–8.

PART II: EXPERIMENTS IN CHRISTIAN DOCTRINE

God. In turning to epistemic questions, Augustine seems to recognize the concern about assurance in verses 13–19, or a desire for the confidence of genuine communion with God.[23] In the face of testing (4:1–3)—including, in Augustine's interpretation, the testing of self-scrutiny—how can one be sure to be acting in devotion to God and not to some other spirit or one's own selfish pride?[24] This is the question of "who God is" expressed under the aspect of personal recognition. 1 John 4:15–16 addresses this question through two restatements of the conditions for abiding in God and God abiding the person: "confess[ing] that Jesus is the Son of God" (v. 15) and "abid[ing] in love" (v. 16b). If Jesus is the Son of God, then Jesus is the very definition of love (4:9–10), so that abiding in love is the same thing as confessing Jesus. As Augustine reasons, to confess Jesus means, "confess[ing], not in word, but in deed, not with the tongue, but with life."[25] Knowing God (and loving God), then, is a way of *living with* the "who" question; one "knows" the answer insofar as one enacts love of neighbor (and, per Augustine, love of enemy), "confessing" Jesus thereby in deed and life (also Titus 1:15–16).[26]

---

23. Augustine, *Tractates*, 8.9, see also 9.10 (cited by homily number and paragraph number, here homily 8, paragraph 9). See also Black, "First, Second, and Third John," 431–32; Lieu, *I, II, and III John*, 194–96; and Marshall, *Epistles of John*, 223–26.

24. Black, "First, Second, and Third John," 431; Augustine, *Tractates*, 8.9–10.

25. Augustine, *Tractates*, 8.14, see also 10.1. The identification of Jesus with the definition of the love-God-is leads Augustine to articulate the concrete form of this love in terms of enemy-love (8.11).

26. See also Maximus the Confessor's argument—partly based on 1 Cor 13:8 ("knowledge, it will come to an end")—that experiential knowledge of God "suspends" conceptual and merely "rational" knowledge; and experiential knowledge is given through *theosis*, participation in the reality of God. Cf. *Cosmic Mystery of Jesus Christ*, 126–27 ("Ad Thalassium 60").

So far this says little more than the ostensive definition of "God" proposed in chapter 3, that God is love, understood as inclusively transcendent. How does the unanswerable (but livable) "who" question involve the Trinity? Riffing on 1 John 4, Augustine senses a trinitarian shape to love itself. When you love the brother or sister whom you see, you also love the love by which you love them.[27] There is the person who loves, the person they love, and the love by which they love. "Love" has a kind of threefold pattern: *I* love, I love *another*, and I love *the love between*. So Augustine can say, "you do see trinity if you see love."[28] This is because the highest love, or "charity," is in itself a dynamic reality with a threefold movement. Although Augustine has emphasized action (confessing Jesus in deed and life), this kind of love doesn't spring from our own innate power. Rather, Augustine encourages us to be responsive to the movement of "charity herself":

> Only let charity herself be present so that we may be moved by her to something good. For when we love charity, we love her loving something, precisely because she does love something. . . . Charity certainly loves itself, but unless it loves itself loving something it does not love itself as charity.[29]

That is, love reflects the Trinity, but not because we can count three things—lover, beloved, and shared love—rather because there's a threefold *pattern of movement* involved in loving, by which human loving participates in God's triune love. The "Trinity" isn't really an *answer* to the who-question but a way of sustaining the who-question faithfully,

27. Augustine, *Trinity*, 8.12.
28. Augustine, *Trinity*, 8.12 (my translation; PL 42:958).
29. Augustine, *Trinity*, 8.12.

PART II: EXPERIMENTS IN CHRISTIAN DOCTRINE

particularly by living out love as a threefold movement that participates in God's threefold relational life (L2).[30]

Does this mean that the Trinity is *only* about the Christian life? Is it a way of using God-talk merely for the sake of saying something about humans? Augustine certainly isn't making that kind of argument, and I don't intend to either. Augustine is writing in the mode of *analogy*, one that fits the idea of analogy articulated in chapter 4 above: using concepts in a systematically ambiguous way to articulate an intellectual judgment about God's reality. The judgment is: *God is love*. More specifically, God is the love of the Father sending the Son (1 John 4:9, 14), the Son who is none other than Jesus's life of love unto atoning death (4:10, 15), and the mutually abiding love given in the Spirit (3:24; 4:13). The argument I'm making through this reading of Augustine doesn't entail that the judgments involved are only *about* human activity; they're *about God*, but they're internal to embodied practices so that their conceptual explication only *works* in connection to a way of life that participates in the reality of which we aim to speak (John 13:31–35).[31] In a life of abiding in God's love, we name God "Father": the love that first loved us and the one from whom the love-that-is-the-Son proceeds; we name God "Son": the love sent by the Father, a love given over in kenotic self-donation; and we name God "Spirit": the abiding reality

---

30. "Love" is not a very fine-grained practice, but this discussion provides something of a grammar or schema within which more specific practices might specify the way of love—practices like forgiveness, hospitality, confession, reconciliation, etc. These are all performances of love; an "ecstatic" way of life given over for the good of others.

31. Cf. Ticciati, *New Apophaticism*, 23–52, 217–46. The way of life in connection with which doctrinal explication of the Trinity "works" is primarily the life of Christian community. Cf. Hauerwas, *With the Grain*, 205–41; and Marshall, *Trinity and Truth*, 182–85, 191–212, 242–75.

of divine love, abiding with Father and Son and drawing creatures into this abiding love.[32]

This way of life is ordered to the content of Jesus's life (1 John 4:10–15) and cannot be sustained in abstraction from continued attention to the concrete details of the New Testament witness (L3). This discussion enriches and specifies the first-personal integration of "grammar" and "metaphysics," inspired by Hildegard and the divine names tradition. By participating in this cruciform way of life, to use Michael Gorman's term (i.e., loving as non-identical repetitions of Christ's kenotic love), we become "analogies" of the Trinity.[33] Or as John and Charles Wesley put it, we become *transcripts* of the Trinity: "Mystically one with thee, / Transcript of the Trinity, / Thee let all our nature own / One in Three, and Three in One."[34] Through participation in God's trinitarian love, we become "secondary analogates" of the Trinity—creaturely love and creaturely holiness don't *cause* the love and holiness of God (in the way that "healthy food" causes the health of the body), but they are *ordered to* God's holy love. God is, to rework an earlier claim, the *final cause* of the (triune) love we analogically perform, so that the potential for love in creatures is realized to the extent that the creature is fulfilled through intimacy with the triune love that God is (integrating L1).[35]

This brings us to the intersection of my Augustinian *praxis*-rooted account of the Trinity and the internal processions according to which God is named. In chapter 4, I

---

32. See Soulen, *Divine Name(s)*, 163–90, who argues that each person of the Trinity enables a distinct pattern of naming God.

33. Gorman, *Cruciformity*, 155–77; and *Inhabiting the Cruciform God*, 85, 105–28.

34. "Communion of the Saints, Part 1," in Wesley, *Hymns and Sacred Poems* (1740).

35. Augustine, *Trinity*, 14.15–16.

presented Maximus the Confessor's christological orientation for divine names as a development on Dionysius's theology. Now, the christological grounding for divine names can be further explored by seeing how it roots God's general procession throughout creation in God's intrinsic processional life.[36] God's "processional life" is revealed in the incarnation. The Word made flesh (John 1:14) "was coming into the world" (1:9b). That is, the Word is "light" proceeding forth into the world, the very light that is the "light of all people.... [It] shines in the darkness, and the darkness did not overtake it" (1:4b–5). Oddly, the world "did not know him," even though it "came into being through him" (1:10, also 1:3). The "Word" about which John speaks seems to be the human Jesus of Nazareth (rather than a "preincarnate" Logos or *logos asarkos*; literally, "Logos without flesh"), though direct reflection on the mystery of incarnation will wait until chapter 6.[37] The event of Jesus's life, death, and resurrection is the "coming into the world" of the light of God—that is, Jesus *proceeds* "from" God and "as" God. And this "procession" is like a light shining into the darkness.

The emanating, processional power of light in connection with the Word led many early theologians to use light-imagery for God and God's intrinsic processions.[38] Gregory of Nazianzus (c. 330–389 CE) is representative of the way light-imagery conveys undivided procession:

---

36. Which means the older language of processions and missions can replace Rahner's Rule and its burden of "two Trinities"; cf. Marshall, "Unity of Triune God," 1–32.

37. Cf. Behr, *John the Theologian*, 1–30.

38. E.g., Augustine, *City of God*, esp. Book 12; Augustine, *Trinity*, 4.5; Dionysius the Areopagite, *Celestial Hierarchy*, 1.2–3; Hilary of Poitiers, *Trinity*, 7.27–29; John of Damascus, *Orthodox Faith*, 1.9; 1.12; 1.17; Aquinas, *ST*, 1.3.7; 1.9.1; 1.12.6–7; Nicholas of Cusa, *God as Not-Other*, chs. 3 and 6.

> We have one God because there is a single Godhead. Though there are three objects of belief, they proceed from the single whole and have reference to it. Neither is one more and another less God, nor one prior and another posterior. ... To express it succinctly, the Godhead exists undivided in beings divided. It is as if there were a single intermingling of light, which existed in three mutually connected suns.[39]

This image vividly captures the paradox of indivisible oneness in distinctive threeness. The "three suns" are undivided from the one light and proceed one to the other in donation of that whole, indivisible light. Or: the three suns just *are* the "proceeding forth" of the entirety of the light itself, so that the light is not divided, diminished, or increased but is "redoubled."[40]

Recently, the image of light has been used for new effect by Linn Marie Tonstad. In *God and Difference*, Tonstad identifies serious deficiencies in the way trinitarian theologians have used gendered language and projected gender-essentialist roles in their characterizations of the triune persons. While these approaches often directly present a male God, some theologians have also engaged in "corrective projectionism"—that is, in an attempt to *avoid* a male God, they project overtly male- *and* female-coded roles onto the relations between Father, Son, and Spirit (in particular masculine "activity" and feminine "passivity").[41] With the intention of *de*literalizing ascriptions of gender to God, corrective projectionism ends up *over*literalizing the

---

39. "Oration" 31.14, in Gregory of Nazianzus, *On God and Christ*, 127 (alt.; PG 36:148D–149A). See also "Oration" 39.11 (*NPNF2* 7:355–56).

40. Emery, *Trinitarian Theology of Aquinas*, 46.

41. Tonstad, *God and Difference*, 13.

gendered conceptual binaries it deploys. Tonstad uses light imagery to capture the unbounded transcendence of God and to articulate a more promising alternative to both a gendered-God and corrective projectionism:

> God is the source of light, and light itself, and the light by which we see.... Were we to look at the divine light directly, we would find darkness and the cloud. If we put light together with dazzling darkness, we find our attempts to start with any one person of the trinity baffled. Instead, we encounter something like an ordered circle: an order in which each person has an irreversible relationship to the others but where relationships are not relations of origin but of intensification or gift.[42]

In line with the account I've developed so far, Tonstad's use of light affirms the impossibility of the direct, unmediated gaze upon God (as Trinity), since it would result in sensory overload. Rather, the "dazzling darkness" of God sets one's eyes in motion, turning from one intensification of light to another. That is, the "light" can't be directly known but is known through following (participating in?) the ordered relations of divine gift.

Tonstad's use of light also helps to integrate Lesson 1 from the exploration of Rahner's Rule, that the mode of knowing depends on God's mode of being. God *is the light* by which we see (Ps 36:9), which is also only known by "seeing" how the light moves in ongoing, mutual gift. The result is that the "persons" simply *are* their relations, so that

---

42. Tonstad, *God and Difference*, 228. I am skeptical of Tonstad's dichotomy between relations of origin and relations of gift or intensification, though I appreciate the latter (see Platter, *Divine Simplicity*, 171–81). Aquinas himself relativizes "origin" by deliteralizing it and by subordinating it to relation in general (Aquinas, *ST*, 1.40.2; 1.28.3, ad 3).

the triune relations are not something other than the one simple "being" of God:

> Each person gifts something to the others, or better, the persons give the same thing in different modes.... The persons (as persons) are nothing aside from their relations to each other.... All give, but in different ways, and those different ways *are* their divine personhood.[43]

This clearly trades on the notion of "procession," so that the triune light consists in the movement of mutual illumination. What distinguishes the trinitarian light by which we see from the creaturely things seen by the light? Or, what's the difference between the threefold processional life intrinsic to God and the manifold creative processions in and through finite beings?

There is nothing "outside" of the intrinsic processions of God: the processions simply *are God* seen in their mutual reference (i.e., each relation is distinct only by reference to the other relations).[44] These relations do not "terminate"—they are each the whole divinity proceeding forth into another relation, fulfilled but not exhausted in being given over to another.[45] By contrast, God's creative processions

43. Tonstad, *God and Difference*, 229.

44. Aquinas, *ST*, 1.27.1: "Careful examination shows that both [Arians and Sabellians] take procession as meaning an *outward act*; hence neither of them affirms procession as existing in God."

45. I haven't explicitly distinguished between "relation" and "procession," which a thorough treatment would more precisely define. In scholastic theology, there's a kind of geometric relation between notion (an abstract name for each triune relation, responding to the "Whereby" question [*Quo sunt tres personae?*]), relation, person, procession, and essence. In God there are *five* notions (Aquinas, *ST*, 1.32.3), *four* relations (1.28.4), *three* persons (1.30.1–2), *two* processions (1.27.3), and *one* essence (1.11.3–4; 1.39.2). It's also worth noting, though, that Aquinas seems to ground relations in

are defined not by reference to another divine relation but by reference to a finite reality. In both cases, a divine procession is a movement of the *entirety* of God, simple, undivided, and replete—in creative processions, this movement is manifest under a creaturely "mask"; in intrinsic processions, this movement is manifest in a pattern of intransitive relationality. We "know" this trinitarian relationality by active participation more fundamentally than by objective description, because the relations don't connect independent beings. Rather, the relations simply are the movement (procession) of the entirety of God, overflowing into the other persons without terminating in a distinct object. We can only know this active, intrinsic self-donation by joining in the movement.

THE LOGICAL PROBLEM: SIMPLY ONE AND THREE PERSONS?

"The answer to the question about the identity of God is for Christian faith, therefore, a triplicity and not a simplicity."[46] As this quotation puts it, God as "simple" and God as "triple" seem like *competing* answers to the question of God's identity. I think the discussion above demonstrates a way to avoid that competitive framing. However, it's still worth asking if simplicity and Trinity are *logically* incompatible, and addressing this question involves making some things explicit that have only been implicit above. How is "simplicity" logically compatible with attributing relations and processions to God? And *what kind* of relations would these be? It seems straightforward to say that anything excluding

---

the processions, so that the kind of priority I've given to procession is fitting even to Aquinas's schematization (cf. Aquinas, *ST*, 1.28.1; Aquinas, *ScG*, 4.26.2–3).

46. Schwöbel, "Trinitätslehre als Rahmentheorie," 33.

intrinsic and extrinsic distinctions can't have relations.[47] Ryan Mullins provides a clear presentation of the problem:

> The Father is intrinsic to God and thus is identical to God's essence and existence. The Son is intrinsic to God and thus identical to God's essence and existence. Identity is transitive [meaning: if a=b and b=c, then a=c], so the Father is identical to the Son, in which case we have no Trinity.[48]

First, let's address the general compatibility between divine simplicity and relationality. While some accounts of simplicity might make God incapable of relations, the account I've developed here doesn't (an account that I think accords with a chorus of thinkers throughout church history). In fact, the initial "metaphysical" framing I put forward was about the exceedingly *inclusive* relation between the many lovers and beloveds in creation and the one God-who-is-love in which they participate. The connection between this construal of inclusive transcendence and divine simplicity consists in the fact that internal and external distinctions are conditions of limited and contrastive relations, so that the simpler something is, the *more* and *more richly* relatable it is.

As the absolutely simple, inclusively transcendent reality, God is *more* relatable because God's unconstrained infinity can be participated in an infinite variety of ways. God is *more richly* relatable because each thing related to God *relates to the entirety of God* (rather than to one part or

---

47. Note the verb "to have" here; recall that according to simplicity, "having" is more accurately converted to "being" ("God *is* what God *has*"). So, we could ask: even if the simple God can't *have* relations, does that mean God can't *be* relations?

48. Mullins in Idol Killer (YouTube Channel), "Divine Simplicity is True."

component of God).⁴⁹ Aquinas says, "it is not unfitting that there be many logical relations in God."⁵⁰ Notice the double negative, "not unfitting."⁵¹ As we learned through the *triplex via*, the way of negation leads to the way of supereminence because the "negation" doesn't express a lack or privation in God. The same goes for intrinsic distinctions: God is not internally or externally differentiated, but the meaning isn't limited to the "not" of "*not* internally differentiated," because it superexceeds the "not" in a divine fullness that transcends such differentiations by the dynamic power to include all differentiated realities. All creatures, though proceeding by act of *will* rather than necessity of nature, do in fact proceed from God and exist in a relation of dependence on God.⁵² Creatures are nothing apart from relation to God, so if that "relation" isn't real, the creature isn't real. God is infinitely relatable because God is not constrained by contrastive definition, internally or externally.⁵³ So my first question—how simplicity is compatible with relations and processions—can be set aside: because unconstrained by contrastive distinctions and superexceeding

---

49. So I agree with Stephen Long that Aquinas's conception of simplicity is always accommodating of relationality; *Perfectly Simple Triune God*, 23–49. Contra Leithart's repeated (and strained) attempts to say otherwise in Leithart, *Creator*, throughout ch. 3.

50. Aquinas, *ST*, 1.32.2. Consider also Sonderegger, *Systematic Theology*, 2:207–10.

51. Space doesn't permit adequately addressing the difference between logical and real relations in scholastic metaphysics. The "logical" qualifier doesn't negate the point being made, since God is infinitely relatable vis-à-vis creation (since creation is really related to God by persistent dependence), and this is "fitting" because of God's inclusive transcendence. I address this in Platter, "Jesus, Trinity, and Creation," 235–39.

52. Aquinas, *ST*, 1.28.1, ad 3; 1.44, preface.

53. Tanner, *God and Creation*, 42–46.

the contrastive domain, God is maximally inclusive and therefore maximally relatable.[54]

But what about the second question, which comes closer to Mullins's critique: what kind of relations are possible for God "internally" and intrinsically without implying separation and essential distinctions? Augustine capitalizes on what seems problematic about relations (namely, reference to another) and turns it into a virtue for the doctrine of the Trinity. A relation is identified *by reference to another*. This means that speaking about God under the aspect of relations is different than speaking about the divine nature as such, because the latter doesn't refer to another like the former does: we say "God is good" or "God is holy" and do so without reference one to the other, so that these claims work as essential divine names. But when one says "Father," this requires reference to another, namely the "Son" of whom the Father is "Father."[55]

A relation points to another, and normally that "other" is an object distinct from the relation—e.g., one sibling is related to another sibling, and each sibling is distinct from their counterpart and the sibling-relation itself. But if there are relations internal to God, these relations, still by "reference to another," do not point to some distinct object. Rather, the relations are related to the other relations. Father *is* the relation of "paternity," which is said of the entirety of God *by reference to* the Son. The Son *is* the relation of "filiation" (or generating-forth) so that the Father's paternity refers not to another "being" but to another relation. And the Spirit *is* the relation of "spiration" (or breathing-forth), a relation to which paternity and filiation refer and that

---

54. Though the adverb "maximally" shouldn't be taken to imply quantity. Cf. Nicholas of Cusa, "Learned Ignorance," 1.23–26; and *God as Not-Other*, chs. 3–5.

55. Augustine, *Trinity*, 5.6; Aquinas, *ST*, 1.28.1–3.

refers back to them in the Spirit's own procession. In this case, God "has" the relation of paternity, because God is named "Father" by reference to the Son. But God "is" whatever God "has." So God—the one, simple, inclusively transcendent God—*is* the reference to another of paternity (and so on for Son and Spirit, *mutatis mutandis*). The relation exists, that is, *as God* rather than "between" separate beings. In Aquinas's terms, the relation *subsists* per se. Divine persons are *subsistent relations*.[56]

This is a strange sounding account of the unity-in-difference of the trinitarian persons, but even if the specifics are hard to grasp, one point can be addressed to Mullins's critique. He invokes the transitivity of identity, which states that if a=b and b=c, then a=c. If water is H2O and H2O is a chemical compound, then water is a chemical compound. This works. Does it work for the Trinity? No, and the reason doesn't require rejecting the general validity of the transitivity of identity or other principles of logic. The names "Father," "Son," and "Spirit" are said to be identical to the divine essence not as one essence would be identical to another, but as *relation* to an *essence* (so we should recall the discussion in chapter 4 on the distinction between the *modus significandi* and the *res significata*). Consequently, the personal names are of a different category than are essential names.[57]

When Mullins says, "The Son is . . . identical to God's essence," the problem is not the *intensity* of the identity-claim—for God the Son *is* the entirety of the divine essence. The problem is that the way "Son" names God differs from the way "divine essence" names God. "Son" names God by reference to another, or *as a relation*, whereas "divine

56. Aquinas, *ScG*, 4.14.6; Aquinas, *ST*, 1.40.2, ad 1; see also 1.28.2; 1.40.1–2.

57. Cf. Aquinas, *ST*, 1.28.3, ad 1; 1.40.1, ad 1.

essence" names God substantially. Consequently, when the Son is said to be identical to God, the Son is not said to be identical to Father or Spirit, since the aspect under which God is named "Son" is by reference to Father and Spirit as *other* at the level of relations.

So: first, I don't think relations as such pose a problem for divine simplicity, so long as simplicity is conceived of as inclusive transcendence. In that view, God is infinitely relatable, because the "lack" of internal essential distinctions is not a matter of privation but of supereminence (per the *triplex via*). Second, all that we know of God is grounded in God's processional life, in which divine procession is an activity or movement of the entirety of God. In one context, this is the pluriform procession of God's perfection in creation (divine names), in another it is the threefold pattern of procession internal to God (Trinity).

God's intrinsic processional life consists of subsistent relations: that is, ways of identifying one triune person by reference to the others without positing some additional "being" or reality "outside" the relation itself. The relation is constituted by reference to the other relations, and each relation names the entirety of the divine essence. So, the persons relate by perichoresis or circumincession, because they are mutually internal to each other (John 14:10–23).[58] And yet the three persons are not identical to each other, and they don't introduce substantial distinctions in God's essence. Rather, the three persons specify the *manner* or

---

58. Butner, *Trinitarian Dogmatics*, 133–51; Torrance, *Doctrine of God*, 169–80. Consequently, the relations are so intimate and mutually internal as to "seem" like identity-relations (as Mullins worries), but because distinguished only *qua* relation, the relations can be entirely coextensive yet not identical without remainder.

mode of God's act. God is pure act according to simplicity, infinitely active without reservation or withholding. *Actus purus* is the act as which the Father eternally generates the Son, the Son generates-forth of the Father (coming into the world as light into darkness), and the Spirit breathes-forth of the Father (and of the Son).

QUESTIONS

1. What are the three variations on Rahner's Rule? What lessons did each provide and how successfully did this chapter integrate them with simplicity?

2. This chapter suggests that knowing the Trinity is a matter of *participation* rather than *description*. Do you agree or disagree?

3. The central claim of this chapter is that God's life is intrinsically processional. Can you restate how this chapter claims that God's life can be intrinsically processional *and* simple?

6

CREATION

And in this vision he also showed a little thing, the size of a hazelnut, lying in the palm of my hand, as it seemed to me, and it was round as a ball.... "It is all that is made." I wondered how it could last, for it seemed to me so small that it might have disintegrated suddenly into nothingness. And I was answered in my understanding, "It lasts, and always will, because God loves it; and in the same way everything has its being through the love of God."

—JULIAN OF NORWICH[1]

IF GOD IS *IPSUM esse*—being-itself in infinite, pure actuality—then everything else depends on God for existence. But can there be a relationship of dependence without subordination and obligatory submission? An episode of the

1. *Revelations*, Long Text, §5.

comedy-drama *Dickinson*, "I Have Never Seen 'Volcanoes,'" poses this question evocatively.[2] In the show's playfully anachronistic style, a young Emily Dickinson is portrayed as subverting social norms and her father's expectations by attending a university lecture about volcanoes disguised as a boy. The episode presents a parallel between Emily's powerful drive to learn and create and the unpredictable power of a volcanic eruption. Just as an eruption can wreak havoc on everything in its vicinity, so also Emily's actions upset her father's sense of order. The story takes an unsettling turn as Emily's mother makes a case for total deference to the father:

Mother   Emily, you need to apologize.

Emily   Apologize? Why should I have to apologize? All I wanted was to just . . .

Mother   Right, well, that is just it, Emily. You only think about what you want. But in this house, what matters is what your father wants. Look around. Everything in this room: that bed, that desk you're sitting at, that pencil you're holding . . . he provided for you. Your father has worked very hard to give us a good life, Emily. So it is my job to keep him happy. And as long as you live under this roof, it is your job too.

Emily tries. She visits the maid and hand-bakes a loaf of bread for her father, who's handling paperwork late into the night. But from here, the volcano symbolism starts to shift. Emily finds that she's not the primary eruptive force in the home but is, instead, caught in another's eruptive, all-consuming grasp. Turning to her friend Sue, she says, "I just can't stop thinking about Pompeii. A whole city covered in ash. Frozen in time. That's how I feel sometimes. Like I'm frozen. Like I'm . . . trapped."

2. Green, *Dickinson*.

Drawing parallels to creation's dependency on the creator isn't difficult. The idea of God explored so far presents such a radical distinction between God and creation that it seems to place all of creation in God's debt. The words of Emily's mother could just as well be said about creature and creator. *What matters is what God wants. Look around. Everything that exists: your world, your friends, your experience, YOU . . . God provided it. So your job is to keep him happy.* Such a God is just as selfish, fragile, and capricious as Emily's father.[3] This is an absent god, a slave-master god, or as Christena Cleveland puts it, "whitemalegod."[4] The plausibility of this parallel poses a deep moral challenge to the doctrine of creation, especially the form that fits with simplicity: creation from nothing (*creatio ex nihilo*).[5] The overall goal of this chapter is to explore the creator–creature relation if God is understood as simple.[6]

A variation on this tension could be put this way: are creatures purely passive and receptive by virtue of their dependence upon God? This is one of the problems diagnosed in the third variation on Rahner's Rule by Moltmann, Jenson, and Jüngel, and it offers a lesson that I noted would need further attention (L4; see fig. 5.1). They argue that construing God as *actus purus* turns God into a panoptic Being exhaustively predetermining everything, so that the realm of creaturely becoming is merely an *expression*

---

3. Sallie McFague calls this the "monarchial model" of God's relation to creation; see *Body of God*, 138–39.

4. Cleveland, *God is a Black Woman*, 22–51.

5. Keller, *On the Mystery*, 47–52. Keller raises this kind of dilemma to reject *creatio ex nihilo*. Compare Baker-Fletcher, *Dancing with God*, 64–73, for whom *ex nihilo* is not proscribed altogether but is rather permitted a playful, midrashic (and perhaps non-literal) role.

6. This framing and many of the convictions guiding this chapter are indebted to Kathryn Tanner's *God and Creation*, with the subtitle, *Tyranny or Empowerment?*

or imperfect *reflection* of what is true and perfect in God. God would be like a movie reel with all of creaturely history pre-recorded and fully contained within God's "protological" actuality. Creatures would exist as predetermined images in God's movie reel, "living" only as the frames of the reel pass through the projector (which is to say, creatures merely *appear* to live rather than actually living).[7] This way of putting it has a logical-philosophical aspect and a moral-theological aspect. The first aspect concerns whether God's pure actuality ends up reducing the apparent contingency of creation into strict necessity—is it the case that even though it seems like things *might have been* otherwise, they can't be? The second concerns whether God is a cosmic tyrant, a capricious patriarch by analogy with Emily's father in *Dickinson*—is it the case that even though things *should* be otherwise, they can't be?

COLLAPSING CREATION INTO NECESSITY?

Can creation be contingent if it's created by a "necessary being"? This logical problem has been forcefully presented by R. T. Mullins, who argues that divine simplicity results in a "modal collapse." In analytic philosophy, "modality" refers to the logic of necessity and possibility. Something is necessary if it *could not* be otherwise (or if it obtains in every "possible world").[8] Something is possible (rather than necessary) if it *could* be otherwise (or if it obtains in at least one but not in all possible worlds).[9] If God is simple, then God is absolutely

---

7. Inspired by Murphy, *God Is Not*, 263–71. However, I use her analogy to characterize the views Jenson critiques, whereas Murphy uses it to characterize Jenson's own views.

8. A "possible world" means the sum of all states of affairs that could obtain together, or the totality of maximally compossible states of affairs; cf. Loux, *Possible and Actual*, 28–36.

9. It's not obvious, however, that the kind of modal logic articulated

necessary. But if God (who is necessary) is identical to God's act, what does this mean for God's *act of creating*? Mullins considers several possibilities: (1) If a simple God creates, God necessarily creates; and if there are multiple "possible worlds," then as a consequence of simplicity's commitment to "pure act," God must have created all possible worlds so that all "possible" worlds are actual (since God is pure act). (2) God might not have created at all, but this would contradict pure actuality, since in this case God would have the *unactualized potential* to create those uncreated worlds. (3) If a simple God creates, God necessarily creates; and if God only creates one "possible world," then the actual world God creates is the only possible world.[10] Mullins considers the first option impossible, because it would require imagining that his individual "essence" exists in multiple possible worlds. The second contradicts divine simplicity from the start. And the third scenario is the "modal collapse," because on this view there are no longer any other possibilities than the one actual world God necessarily creates—and therefore the difference between necessity and possibility has been collapsed. This is the one Mullins thinks the logic of divine simplicity and pure actuality requires. However, it too is internally contradictory, Mullins argues, because it secures God's pure actuality at the cost of God's "aseity," since God is only "pure act" as long as there is a world God creates. That implies that God's pure actuality depends on the existence of the world, which in the end conflicts with the meaning of pure act itself.[11]

---

by "possible worlds" semantics has validity for the God–world relation. For a compelling critique of using such modal logic for analyzing the God–world relation from the perspective of participatory metaphysics, see Griffiths, *Intellectual Appetite*, 80–91.

10. Mullins, "Simply Impossible," 194–96.
11. Mullins, "Simply Impossible," 196.

However, the first and third options both take a set of entailments from simplicity as axiomatic, and the arguments depend on the validity of the purported entailments. This set of entailments was expressed in my summary as: if a simple God creates, God *necessarily* creates. In another context, Mullins presents an argument for this claim:

> On divine simplicity God's essence is identical to His existence. Also, God's one simple act is identical to His essence/existence. God's act of creation is identical to this one simple act, and so identical to God's essence/existence. God exists of absolute necessity. So His act of creation is of absolute necessity since it is identical to His essence/existence.[12]

If God is God's act (as simplicity claims), and if God creates by divine act, then the act of creation is identical to the pure act God is. Therefore, if God exists of necessity, the act of creation also exists of necessity. If this is correct, then the axiomatic entailments undergirding arguments one and three above are vindicated: if a simple God creates, God necessarily creates. The challenge of this argument is serious, since it would not only mean that God must create, but it would also mean (per argument three) that *this* specific created world is necessary, down to every last detail. Indeed, nothing in the created universe would be contingent or possibly otherwise, for it would all have been determined by necessity from God's all-inclusive act of creation. The fears expressed above, in the *Dickinson* analogy and the summary of the theologians of hope, would be confirmed.[13]

The primary entailment is that a simple creator necessarily creates. Because Mullins's argument depends on

---

12. Mullins, *Timeless God*, 138.

13. E.g., Hinlicky, *Divine Simplicity*, 19–24, uses Mullins's argument against Thomistic doctrines of God.

analytic-style conceptions of modality, it needs to be assessed for its validity in those terms. Christopher Tomaszewski convincingly exposes a serious weakness in Mullins's use of modal operators. Following his lead, let's put the argument in its simplest form:

1. Necessarily, God exists.
2. God is identical to God's act of creation.
3. Necessarily, God's act of creation exists.[14]

This looks like a valid argument, and according to divine simplicity, the first two premises are true. However, Tomaszewski argues that the conclusion doesn't follow, because it makes a fundamental error in modal logic—i.e., an "invalid substitution into modal contexts."[15] He shows why this is the case by reference to another argument of the same form:

1* Necessarily, $8 > 7$
2* Number of the planets $= 8$
3* Necessarily, the number of the planets > 7.[16]

The flaw of this argument isn't hard to see, even if an explanation of its error takes some effort. In these arguments, a truth relative to one possible world or one "modal context"—in 1–3*, that the number of planets equals eight in our world—is substituted into a truth-claim that purports to apply to *all* possible worlds (some of which might only have 5 planets in our solar system, or none). Returning to our primary focus (the act of creation), the "substitution" happens when one takes a truth that contains a reference

---

14. Tomaszewski, "Collapsing the Modal Collapse," 277.
15. Tomaszewski, "Collapsing the Modal Collapse," 278–79.
16. Tomaszewski, "Collapsing the Modal Collapse," 278 (my paraphrase).

to the product of God's creative act, thereby assuming the context in which that created world exists, and applies it to God in a more generic modal context—viz., a context that doesn't specify the created world by reference to which God's act of being can be called a creative act. Because this substitution is invalid, it doesn't support the conclusion that the necessity proper to God's pure actuality can be attributed to the act of creation. This counterargument is similar to the one offered on the doctrine of the Trinity: the entirety of God is named "creator" but under the aspect of a specific relation, namely, by reference to the created world. If the meaning of "God's act" is different when referring to its eternal actuality than when referring to its product, the created world, then it isn't amenable to the same modal operator in both cases. Consequently, the dilemma Mullins introduced above doesn't arise. In terms of modal semantics, it doesn't seem like a "modal collapse" is a serious risk.

However, all of this operates primarily at the level of semantics, or how words (like "necessity") are used.[17] So let's ask the question in a way that is less concerned with "modal semantics" and more concerned with the *manner* of God's creative activity. How does it actually *work* that God creates the world without exhaustively determining it and collapsing the breadth of possibility into mere necessity? And is that manner of creating compatible with divine simplicity?

CONSTRUING THE CREATOR–CREATURE RELATION

I think there are two ways of contextualizing the act of creation that support a non-deterministic rendering: first, there is a vital distinction between primary and secondary agency (referred to as "double agency"). Second, we could

17. Cf. Mullins's response in Mullins and Byrd, "Simplicity and Modal Collapse," 33–38. But for expanded discussion and critique, see Tomaszewski, "Simple Creator Escapes," 238–47.

imagine God's creative act by analogy with "final causation," in which case God might be able to create for a specific end without determining in every detail the ways creatures move toward that end. These considerations will help address the moral-theological concern of whether God is a cosmic tyrant.

Double agency is an attempt to formally express the way that God's action to *produce* the created world operates at a different level than creaturely causation (either in self-determination, as in free human action; or in "efficient causation," when one thing brings about a change in another). In exploring Mullins's modal collapse argument above, a crucial term was "God's act of creation." This phrase, however, is ambiguous—does "God's act of creation" refer to the act by which God creates or the act of being (esse) proper to creatures (recall the discussion of analogy and the *analogia entis* in chapter 4)? Mullins's argument seems to collapse or ignore any possible distinction between the two, but "double agency" offers a formalization of the analogical relationship between God's act of creating and creation's act of being/becoming. Double agency has its home in a doctrine of *creatio ex nihilo* (creation from nothing). To say that God creates *ex nihilo* is to specify the manner of God's creative action—it's not primarily about a first moment in time or about the relative insubstantiality of creation. In what follows, I assume Ian McFarland's construal of *ex nihilo*. Following Anselm, McFarland rejects adjectival interpretations of *ex nihilo* (which tend to assume that "nothing" names some state, like moment before creation, or some kind of reality, like "nothingness" or a quantum vacuum). Instead, McFarland advocates an adverbial interpretation: "from nothing" qualifies *the manner of God's creative act*. He explicates this in three statements: creation is grounded in *nothing but* God, there exists *nothing apart from* God, and in God's creative act *nothing limits* God.[18]

Some assessments of God's all-encompassing creative power seem to imply that God is *the* only cause of every aspect of creation, which results in divine "omnicausality" (and Mullins's critiques would be appropriate against this view). Double agency challenges this inference by first suggesting that God doesn't "cause" creation in the way creatures causally interact with one another. Further, while God's creative agency is exhaustive and immediate, this is rooted in the utterly unique *manner* of God's agency. Austin Farrer (1904–1968) uses the ocean analogy in the language of surface and depth to capture this difference:

> These [diverse causal relations amongst finite beings] connect, as it were, the several parts of a surface; the new relation [borne by the infinite creator] gives the backing in depth which this surface, as a surface, must have.[19]

As creator, God acts as existence-itself to that which must *receive* existence from another. And this can be expressed by analogy with the relation of depth to surface. John of Damascus (c. 675–749 CE), in his *Exposition of the Orthodox Faith*, deploys the image of an ocean or sea to express the immensity of God's simple mode of being. In Book 1, chapter 9, John defends the simplicity of God, according to which God is nameless but receives names from all creaturely reality (recall chapter 4 above). He then turns to reflect on the name "THE ONE WHO IS," invoking at that moment the image of the ocean: "[God] keeps all being in his own embrace, like a sea of essence infinite and unbounded."[20]

---

18. McFarland, *From Nothing*, 86–107.

19. Farrer, *Finite and Infinite*, 22.

20. John of Damascus, *Orthodox Faith*, 1.9 (*NPNF*2 9:12, alt.; PG 94:835/836B).

Creation

The image of "a sea of essence" expresses three things about God: (1) God holds all things in the divine embrace, (2) God is infinite, and (3) God is unbounded. Part of the power of imagining God to be ocean-like is the way it specifies the significance of "unbounded" (sometimes translated as "unseen"). It is not that God is absent, opposed to locality, or even intangible; rather, God is unbounded precisely in the sense that God is all-encompassing and pervasive. God is unbounded or "unseen" to creatures, like the way a fish might frantically swim around trying to "find the ocean."[21]

We might be inclined to think of God as ocean-container and creatures as inhabitants of the ocean—and this "container" use of the image vividly captures the divine embrace. But in light of Farrer's quotation and the double-agency question, we might instead think of the ocean image in terms of depth (Ps 36:6–7; Rom 11:33). The whole of creation is the flux and refraction at play on the ocean's surface. We interact and affect each other as creatures because these interactions all take place on the "horizontal plane" of the real. However, the surface is not the whole; rather, it is suspended by the "vertical plane" of the ocean's depth. The surface is real and dynamically interactive, but its reality and activity are only possible because the surface is "suspended" by the ocean depths. Through this lens, God's embrace of creation is of a different order, sustaining creaturely interaction and causation by the "primary act" of donating existence.

Thinking in terms of a horizontal and a vertical plane draws attention to the non-competitive difference between God and creation, connecting God's primary act to creation's own genuine secondary activity. And when paired with the adjective "infinite," it evokes God's (vertical) difference through the lens of supereminence (like the

21. Wallace, "This Is Water."

culminating moment in the *triplex via*), which expresses the inclusive transcendence of God. John Wesley uses the ocean image to articulate the path of human perfection: "The sea is an excellent figure of the fulness of God, and that of the blessed Spirit. For as the rivers all return into the sea; so the bodies, the souls, and the good works of the righteous, return into God, to live there in his eternal repose."[22] The human is perfected by being drawn into God's water-like life, and this "return" involves body, soul, and "good works" (Isa 58:11; John 7:37–39; Eph 5:26–27; Rev 21:6).

The import of the analogy is that God actively creates, but not by exerting force on creatures in the way one creature acts on another. God's creative act brings about and sustains the order of being within which creatures interact. Consequently, God's action is compatible with the genuine interaction of creatures because God's action is of a more fundamental sort. Creatures act by secondary causation, exerting influence on other things that already exist. God's primary act brings it about that there *is anything at all* that can be changed and influenced.[23]

The capacity of creatures to interact causally by their own agency is an outflow of the specific kind of act that God's act of creation is (Gen 1:20–25). In creating "from nothing" God *gives existence-itself* to that which otherwise would not exist. God's gift of existence is a *self-communicative* gift, so that God gives creatures their own *power to self-communicate*. As W. Norris Clarke puts it,

> Not only is activity, active self-communication, the natural consequence of possessing an act

---

22. Wesley, *Plain Account*, 146 (Jackson, 11:435; Bicentennial, 13:124).

23. So Aquinas argues that God's act of creation isn't a kind of "change" since there is nothing independent of the act that goes from one state to another; Aquinas, *ST*, 1.45.1, ad 2; 1.45.2, ad 2.

of existence (*esse*); St. Thomas goes further to
maintain that self-expression through action is
actually the whole point, the natural perfection
or flowering of being itself, the goal of its very
presence in the universe.[24]

This is what it means to say that God is the "primary agent" or the "depth" to creation's "surface"—God creates by giving existence, and existence (*esse*) is the power to communicate. In this way, creaturely existence possesses its own relative and contingent power to "flower" into being, i.e., to act in self-expressive, self-communicative, and self-determining ways. Creaturely self-communication is "secondary act," because even while this activity is genuine and proper to the creature, it remains dependent on God's "primary act" in giving *esse*. And yet, in "giving" existence, God doesn't *determine* the details of creatures' existence, because the existence God gives is the active power of *esse* by which creatures self-actualize through self-communicative action.

Creaturely activity, then, is a kind of movement, the realization through time and mutual interaction of creatures' own intrinsic possibilities.[25] This kind of action has an open teleological orientation, a direction of travel that is pregnant with various possibilities for flourishing and various ways of failing to flourish (Pss 19:2–4; 104:27–30; 148; Prov 8:22–36; 16; Eccl 2:18–26; Matt 6:26–30). This naturally transitions to a final-cause analogy for the act of creation: God doesn't create by pushing things into predetermined slots or by running a pre-recorded movie reel through a projector; rather God opens up a horizon for creaturely movement towards an end—and in one sense, God simply *is* this end (Gen 1:31–2:3; Prov 16:33; Rev

---

24. Clarke, *Explorations in Metaphysics*, 213.
25. McFarland, *From Nothing*, 63–65, 142–52.

21:22–26; 22:5; 22:13).²⁶ Within this framing, I think we can imagine a creaturely autonomy that moves away from the capricious, patriarchal image of an all-possessive God.

Aquinas argues that God is the "first mover" or "unmoved mover"—somewhat unattractive descriptors for God.²⁷ But implicit in this characterization is the idea that God's creative activity is *intentionally ordered*; that is, God is not a force *pushing* things into motion but is, rather, intimately active in and through the ordered sequence of movements within creation and attracting creatures toward an end.²⁸ God is creation's "first mover" by donating existence (primary act) and, in the same act, by moving creatures toward their perfection or fruition (final cause). God "moves" creatures in this way by accompanying them in their own movement (their secondary activity). We have to consider once again the "modal collapse," but now in a different context. If God's action is the ultimate final cause of creaturely ordered activity, and if God's final causation operates by drawing all things to God as their end, doesn't this reduce the apparent diversity of creaturely potential

---

26. E.g., Nicholas of Cusa, "Learned Ignorance," 1.23; Aquinas, *ST*, 1.103.2.

27. Aquinas, *ST*, 1.2.3, the "first way."

28. The series of movements that "cannot go on to infinity" in Aquinas's "argument from motion" is an intrinsically ordered series (*per se*) rather than an extrinsically ordered series (*per accidens*). Consider Aquinas's example of a hand as mover of a staff: independently of the continuous, accompanying motion of the hand, the staff doesn't move—the series of movers are intrinsically ordered to one another. An intrinsically ordered series requires a "source" of its motion, otherwise the principle animating the whole series would be lacking, and, hence, there would be no intrinsically ordered series at all. However, for this to "prove" the existence of God depends on whether one sees finite motions "as" a *per se* series rather than *per accidens*. So, it depends on the "dawning of an aspect" or "seeing as," to use Wittgenstein's phrases (*Philosophical Investigations*, Part II, §113, §118).

into a singular predetermined actuality? If creation has only *one end*—namely God—doesn't that mean that creaturely movement is predetermined, that there aren't *multiple possible ends* of creaturely development because they all collapse into the same end, God?

Aquinas himself considers a variation on this question, asking whether the "effects" of God's providence (God's activity, as I put it above, to "attract" creatures toward an end) are many or one, and he concludes that the effects are many. There are, he says, three aspects to creaturely perfection/fulfillment.[29] First, there is the ultimate good-itself to which creatures are ordered for their fulfillment, and this is God alone. Second, creatures can imitate God by acting for the good of others, accompanying other creatures in movement toward the good (both as humans accompany other creatures [Gen 1:26–28; Rom 8:19–22] and as nonhuman creatures accompany humans [Ps 19:1–4; Isa 55:10–13]).[30] Third, there is the particular creaturely goodness proper to each, and this is the creature's own flourishing as the unique creature it is (Pss 104; 148; Isa 35:1–2; 44:23; 55:12–13). The first aspect is singular, but the other two are numerous. Because the second and third permit not only diversity of creaturely ends "without number," as Aquinas says, but also an infinite variety of *means* to those ends (how unfathomably numerous are the ways one creature might accompany another in pursuing the good?), God's "final causality" is compossible with an infinite diversity of creaturely ends and means to those ends.

Putting together the primary/secondary agency distinction and the compossibility of diverse creaturely ends ("without number") with the one end-God-is, we can finally lay the "modal collapse" critique to rest. God is the simple

29. Aquinas, *ST*, 1.103.4.

30. Also Aquinas, *ScG*, 3.70.7. For the exegetical points, see Bauckham, *Bible and Ecology*, 64–102, on the "community of creation."

act by which creatures receive their act of existence (*esse*), the power to *self*-communicate and *self*-direct; and in that one act, God accompanies creatures in their own proper movement toward flourishing, attracting them to the singular and simple goodness of God's being (Rev 21:23–26). As the inclusively transcendent final cause, God is infinitely relatable and infinitely realizable in the numerous finite ends to which creatures move.

This now makes it possible to address the moral question directly, the seeming caprice of a God who is the exhaustive source and singular end of creaturely existence. I've been suggesting that God is the "end" of creatures, analogous to "final causation." At one level, this bears resonance with Emily's mother as she justifies passive, obligatory obedience by reference to the father's all-encompassing possessiveness. But the account I've been developing suggests an important disanalogy in God's relationship to creatures. The crucial difference lies with the claims that God accompanies creatures in their own movement and that God does so as an inclusively transcendent "final cause" sustaining an infinite variety of creaturely forms of flourishing.

The "job" of a creature then can be understood *both* as ordered to God's goodness and as ordered to the creature's own goodness, noncompetitively (Prov 16:31). Andrew Davison draws out this element of Aquinas's thought by noting the intrinsic dynamism of creaturely "form." "Form" in Aquinas's thought is similar to "logos" in Maximus's thought—it is the intelligible or "logical" structure of a finite being (discussed in chapter 4). Aquinas thinks of form as "*something divine* . . . divine because every form is a certain participation by likeness of the divine being, which is pure act."[31] In this framing, then, a creature is not meant to be

---

31.. Aquinas, *Commentary on Aristotle's Physics,* 1.15.135 (quoted in Davison, *Participation in God,* 116).

extrinsically deferential to God, rather each creature's *telos* is to be *like God* in itself: "like God," Davison says, "in the sense of realizing what it belongs to that particular creature to be—in realising [sic] what it is of God that it, specifically, can realize."[32]

Being fulfilled in "godlikeness" is, then, not primarily an act of deference and self-abasement. On the contrary, godlikeness is the fruit of flourishing as the particular creature one is.[33] Here, in sum, is the decisive difference between Emily's father and the understanding of God according to simplicity: Emily's father needed her to defer to him by *restricting her own intrinsic capacities*, and only in that way could she have her "proper place" in *his* world; with God, by contrast, intrinsic capacity and godlikeness are not in competition.[34] On the contrary, a creature draws nearer to God and glorifies God precisely by flourishing in its own particularity and by accompanying other creatures in their movements toward flourishing. And this suggests that creatures do in fact possess their own integrity and relative autonomy.

Creatures are not mere passive puppets of the "protological simplicity" of God; they are active subjects of their own

32. Davison, *Participation in God*, 117.

33. This doesn't mean that flourishing is free of suffering or is a kind of "cheap grace." Rather, flourishing has a christological form that requires integration with an account of kenosis and "cruciformity." One way to allude to such integration is to note that creaturely particularity is also a function of mutual interconnectedness, so that flourishing is not the goal of a private individual but lies in the often costly pursuit of shared good(s).

34. Christena Cleveland's articulation of God's "deep power" is a vital challenge to the monarchial vision of God; cf. *God Is a Black Woman*, 48–49, 154.

proper movement opened up and sustained by the inclusively transcendent God in whom creaturely particularity has its own self-communicative and self-actualizing power. Far from being *compromised* by thinking of God as "simple," the account of simplicity I've been developing positively contributes to this affirmation of creaturely integrity and active self-direction. This God-who-is-love (*simply* love) is known through the messy, often vulnerable, and contingent work of living into one's vocation to love: to love the specific creature one is, thereby moving toward integrity, wholeness, and flourishing; to love one's creaturely neighbors, accompanying them in their unique movement toward flourishing; and to love (in all these loves) the God who is infinitely lovable and so noncompetitively loved and loving.

QUESTIONS

1. Why might creation from nothing raise moral questions? Are there other concerns you would raise for creation from nothing?

2. Can you summarize the modal collapse critique of simplicity? How successful is Tomaszewski's response?

3. The chapter explores double-agency and the analogy of God as final cause (*telos*). Do these ideas successfully avoid both a "modal collapse" and a patriarchal-monarchial view of God?

7

INCARNATION

I saw that the same beloved Second Person who is our mother in our substantial being has become our mother in our sensory being; for we are twofold by God's making, that is to say, in substance and sensory being. . . . And so our mother—in whom the parts of us are kept undivided—works within us in various ways; for in our mother, Christ, we profit and grow, and in mercy he reforms and restores us, and, by virtue of his Passion and his death and resurrection, he unites us to our substance.

—JULIAN OF NORWICH[1]

"CHRIST OUR MOTHER"—IN THIS phrase, Julian conveys a soteriology and a Christology in one. Jesus Christ, the "Second Person" of the Trinity, joins our "twofold" nature (i.e., substantial and sensory) and restores us. Keeping our own

1. *Revelations*, Long Text, §58.

parts "undivided," Christ nurtures in us a kind of simplicity proper to our human creatureliness through union with God our mother (who is pure, unbounded, undividedness, i.e., simple). Julian's mothering Christ is the all-sustaining God of creation—always-already bearing creation in its "substantial being"—and this same Christ *becomes* our human mother, bearing our "sensory being" in passion, death, and resurrection (John 15:4–15; Rom 6:4–8). Our mother Christ rebirths us into relative "simplicity" and peace, knitting back together what we restlessly unravel (Luke 13:34; Eph 2).[2]

In *The Kindness of God*, Janet Martin Soskice suggests that for Julian, Christ is quintessentially "kind," which says more than our twenty-first century English might lead us to assume.

> In Middle English the words "kind" and "kin" were the same—to say that Christ is "our kinde Lord" is not to say that Christ is tender and gentle, although that may be implied, but to say that he is kin—our kind. This fact, and not emotional disposition, is the rock which is our salvation.[3]

Christ is "our kinde Lord," which is another way to say that Christ is our mother: Christ joins our "kind," and now, in him, we are made "kin." A deep paradox undergirds this incarnational soteriology: the infinite, simple God becomes our "kind," our "kin," and in this way we finite, composite creatures become God's kin (John 1:12; Rom 8:14–17).

---

2. Julian, *Revelations*, Long Text, §49. Anselm also says, "And you, Jesus, are you not also a mother? / Are you not the mother who, like a hen, gathers her chickens under her wings? / Truly, Lord, you are a mother; for both they who are in labour and they who are brought forth are accepted by you. / . . . It is by your death that they have been born, for if you had not been in labour, you could not have borne death; / and if you had not died, you would not have brought forth" ("Prayer to St. Paul," 153).

3. Soskice, *Kindness of God*, 5.

The Word made flesh—Christ bearing us in his flesh—is the heart of Christian faith. As such, it is a mystery that exceeds words (John 21:25), even while proclaiming this Word is the central task of Christian witness (1 Cor 1:23, 2:1–2; Gal 6:17; Eph 3). Proclaiming the Word made flesh is a challenge, not only because of the immensity of the mystery but also because of the apparent mismatch between our image(s) of God and the historical event of incarnation. How do we make sense of the eternal God undergoing birth, growth and maturation, ministry, suffering, crucifixion, death, resurrection, and ascension? The incarnation is the vital heart of the gospel but, by connection with change and finitude, it seems incompatible with simplicity. If that's right, then simplicity is finally incompatible with the gospel, and therefore doesn't belong to Christian doctrine.

This apparent mismatch can be expressed in two questions. Can we think of the eternal Word, the Logos, as "impassible" and uphold the unity of divinity and humanity in the suffering of Jesus? And if the humanity of God is active—not a mere puppet of the Word's manipulation—should we think of the incarnation (the union of humanity and divinity) as symmetrical or asymmetrical? The first question concerns the so-called *logos asarkos* (the preincarnate Word) and the kenosis (self-emptying/self-giving) of the incarnate Christ (Phil 2:7). Here I dialogue with Robert Jenson. The second question concerns the "communication of attributes" between the divine and human natures of Christ—that is, does the union of the two natures change or add to human nature? Does it change or add to divine nature? Here I enter into dialogue with Bruce McCormack's kenotic Christology and the recent work on Maximus the Confessor by Jordan Daniel Wood. These two questions build on each other and are, in some ways, just different vantage points on the same dynamic: how Christ is our divine-human mother. I argue that simplicity does benefit (indirectly) some of these crucial moves. Most importantly for present purposes, these dialogues aim to show that Jenson and McCormack wrongly blame simplicity in their diagnoses of christological errors.

TWO NATURES, ONE HYPOSTASIS

First, let me introduce some christological terms that will play a crucial role in what follows. The most fundamental distinction is between nature (*physis* or *ousia*) and "person" (*hypostasis*). We have encountered this distinction already, especially in chapter 5 on the Trinity. There I pointed to the fundamental difference between the unanswerable "what" question and the unanswerable "who" question. The first concerns a "nature" the second concerns "personhood." In this chapter, however, the use of "person" is especially fraught with risks, because we often think of consciousness or mind as the person, but this is not helpful for understanding the historic debates around Christology. For this reason, I'll use the untranslated "hypostasis" to refer to the "who" of Christ rather than the word "person."

In the chart on the facing page (fig. 7.1), I represent the "christological heresies" on two axes. On the *x*-axis, a view could be plotted according to how its affirmation of one nature seems to come at the expense of the other: at the extremes, Docetism affirms the divinity at the expense of the "full humanity" and Adoptionism (Ebionite) affirms the humanity at the expense of the "full divinity." On the *y*-axis, a view could be plotted according to the mode of union between the natures: Nestorianism affirms two complete natures that seemingly exist parallel to one another in different "subjects" or hypostases, whereas Eutychianism blends the two natures into a single hybrid. Chalcedon aims to avoid all these extremes by affirming full divinity and full humanity (rejecting the extremes on the *x*-axis) and by specifying the manner of the union as "hypostatic," viz., both natures belong to one hypostasis, without separation or confusion (rejecting the extremes on the *y*-axis).

So, according to the Chalcedonian definition, the one hypostasis, the eternal Logos (or God the Son) has two natures without confusion, without change, without division, and without separation.[4] All that it is to be human, including temporal beginning and end, a human mind, and a human will, is predicated of the one hypostasis. And all that it is to be divine (*ipsum esse*, pure actuality, infinity, etc.) is predicated of one and the same hypostasis. What's more, the divinity of the Son *is not changed* (viz., remains "immutable") in the hypostatic union, and this commitment at Chalcedon seems dependent upon commitment to divine simplicity. However, it's not only the divine nature that remains unchanged in the incarnation, for the human nature is also "without change."

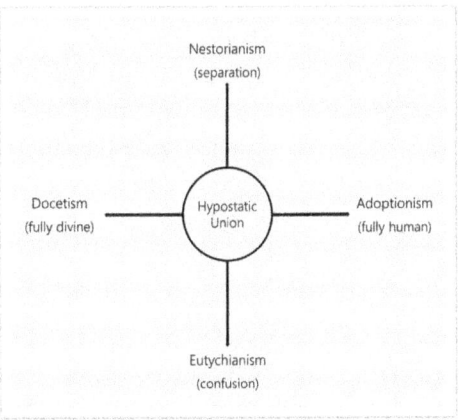

Fig. 7.1—Chart of the Four Major Christological Heresies

4. Tanner, *Decrees*, 86.

PART II: EXPERIMENTS IN CHRISTIAN DOCTRINE

THE IMPASSIBLE LOGOS AND THE SUFFERING JESUS?

The idea of the "preincarnate" Logos (*logos asarkos*) has been the source of controversy in modern theology, especially in the wake of Karl Barth's (1886–1968) critique and nuanced affirmation.[5] A central concern could be captured by Rowan Williams's justly famous claim that "the existence of Jesus is not an episode in the biography of the Word."[6] The Son isn't an infinitely long life-story in which Jesus plays a short, supporting role (John 8:58; Eph 1:4). If *logos asarkos* means that the Word temporally pre-exists and post-exists the life of Jesus, then Williams rejects this notion.[7] But is Williams committed, then, to the idea that God *becomes* Trinity at the same moment that Jesus is born of Mary Theotokos? Would God otherwise have been unipersonal (just "Father") or dipersonal (just "Father" and "Spirit")?

Some people think Robert Jenson (1930–2017) says something like that when he argues that the Son's "eternal generation" from the Father just is the same event as Jesus's birth from Mary.[8] In his *Systematic Theology*, he says that the "antecedence" of the Word is a narrative pattern within Israel that prefigures or anticipates Jesus's birth from Mary: "the Son appears as a narrative pattern of Israel's created human story before he can appear as an individual Israelite within that story."[9] What kind of "narrative pattern" does Jenson have in mind, and how could that both be an eternal

---

5. Most concisely in Barth, *CD*, IV/1, 52–53.

6. Williams, *Arius*, 244.

7. See James Cone's critique of "Logos christology" (i.e., a Christology that tries to start from an unincarnate Logos) for the ways it abstracts from the particulars of Jesus's life in ways that uphold the political status quo. *God of the Oppressed*, 99–126.

8. Jenson, "Once More."

9. Jenson, *Systematic Theology*, 1:141.

antecedence *and* belong to the historical event of the incarnation? In that same text, Jenson tries to clarify:

> In the triune life, what ontologically precedes the birth to Mary of Jesus who is God the Son . . . is the narrative pattern of *being going to be* born to Mary. What in eternity precedes the Son's birth to Mary is not an unincarnate state of the Son, but a pattern of movement within the event of the Incarnation, the movement to incarnation, as itself a pattern of God's triune life.

Divine simplicity seems incompatible with this way of putting it. If the Logos is "antecedent" only as a narrative pattern definitionally ordered to an historical event, then the Son's divine reality depends on a creaturely reality. According to simplicity, God is eternally *pure act*, without any passive potentiality (see chapter 3), which would mean that the Son's *divinity* is also pure act and so doesn't depend on a creaturely event to "actualize" some passive potency (e.g., the anticipated potential "to be born to Mary"). From Jenson's perspective, all the worse for such a doctrine of simplicity: if the gospel demands speaking this way about the Word's union with an historic event, then those who proclaim the gospel must reject anything that inhibits such speech, including an "unbaptized" simplicity.

In Jenson's own proposal, however, he self-consciously deploys something of the logic of simplicity while critically rejecting what he considers "unbaptized" vestiges of the concept. How can God the Son "precede" birth to Mary without becoming something separate from Jesus? The answer, for Jenson, bears remarkable similarities to the trinitarian concepts developed in chapter 5 on the Trinity, namely a triune person isn't "some*thing*" but is a *subsistent relation*. In the triune life, "persons" *just are the relations* according to which God self-relates, without anything existing "outside" the relations (see ch. 5). So, the eternal Logos "precedes" birth to Mary not as "some*thing*" separate from Jesus but as a divine relation, a procession or movement internal to the divine life.[10] So far, Jenson's logic seems to fit well with divine simplicity.

Jenson's way of handling this "movement" internal to God is by defining it as a narrative pattern directed toward an historical event (birth to Mary). Here Jenson depends on a future-oriented metaphysics. God acts on history by actualizing God's life through eschatological anticipation, or advent. God "is" eternally what God "will be" as that future is opened up by the Spirit of freedom.[11] So, in Jenson's mind, God can be defined by an event in time (even a relatively "future" event) because God's unity is (always/eternally) achieved through the advent of the future. This resolves a christological tension for Jenson, a lesson that I hope to integrate as well, namely that the historical life of Jesus is properly honored as the genuinely *human* life of God. The postulate of a *logos asarkos* would, in Jenson's mind, make Jesus a purely passive "reflection" or Platonic shadow of the ideal reality (an unincarnate Logos). The incarnation would then be Docetic in form (the Logos playacting as though human) and would also be a ladder to kick away once the destination had been reached (i.e., knowledge of the divine reality itself, without flesh). But by identifying the Son exclusively with the historical event of incarnation, actualized by the advent of the Spirit, Jenson avoids treating Jesus as a pre-recorded movie reel (fully actualized in the Son's primordial eternity) that is merely projected outward onto the world stage.[12] That is, Jesus isn't just a passive humanity that the Son simply instrumentalizes,

10. Jenson, "Once More," 124.
11. Jenson, *Systematic Theology*, 1:156–61.
12. See the discussion of this analogy in the previous chapter.

because in that case the suffering and passion of Jesus would not really be God the Son's suffering, and we'd end up not only with Docetism but also with marks of Nestorianism (two subjects of the events of incarnation).

However, Jenson integrates this lesson at severe cost, and I worry he does so at risk of a different christological error. First, Jenson's futurist ontology is at best mind-bendingly counterintuitive and at worst problematic Christian/metaphysical grammar. This alone is worth further exploration.[13] However, homing in on the christological matter, Jenson courts a Eutychian-like Christology. My concern is that in his desire to fully affirm the humanity of Jesus, Jenson ends up trying to ground the *unity* of the two natures *in the natures*. As I summarized above, neither the divine nature nor the human nature *changes* through the union, which means that it's fruitless to point to events or aspects of the human nature for "clues" of the divine nature. To look to the human nature in this way would presuppose that some such change had taken place, that the human nature or narrative itself would disclose or constitute the divine *nature*. Jenson tends in just this way to look to the human nature for a clue to the divine-human union, and this ends up locating the unity at the level of the natures themselves so that something of the divine gets altered to fit the human.[14] In this case, Jesus appears to be a hybrid—ideally a

---

13. I attempt such an exploration in Platter, *Divine Simplicity*, esp. 104–35.

14. I consider this to be an instance of what McFarland calls the "Leonine temptation," after Pope Leo I's Tome, in which Leo points to Jesus's miracles as a function of the divine nature and his suffering as a function of his humanity ("Spirit and Incarnation," 146–49). While sympathetic to much of Jenson's theology, Bruce McCormack also resists this move in his kenotic Christology, saying that the Word remains immutable but *not* impassible (*Humility*, 178–86).

bit more human-like than Christians often affirm, but worryingly hybrid-like nonetheless.

If, as simplicity seems to require, the divine nature doesn't change in the Word's union with human nature, then the union in question shouldn't require the human nature to change either.[15] In this case, what happens? In the incarnation, the whole life of Jesus of Nazareth, with all its human particularity from conception to death, resurrection, and ascension, has God the Son as its "who," as the hypostatic subject of that life. There is no one else to whom this life belongs, no separate human "who" or hypostasis. As Ian McFarland argues, this means that Jesus's divine difference from other humans is exactly the same as the difference between any *non*-divine humans—it is the difference of hypostasis, or of the singular subject of the distinctly human life each human lives.[16] The union is entirely at this level. God the Son, the eternal second person of the Trinity, is the only personal subject of Jesus's human life. As such, God the Son is a divine hypostasis, an intrinsic procession of the (simple) entirety of God, consubstantial (*homoousion*) with the Father, and this same hypostasis is consubstantial (*homoousion*) with humanity, bearing a strictly human life as his own.[17]

At this point we can return to Rowan Williams's quotation in its entirety: "The Word as God is the condition of there being a human identity which is the ministering, crucified and risen saviour, Jesus Christ; but the existence of Jesus is not an episode in the biography of the Word."[18] His celebrated phrase does indeed deny a temporally preexistent *logos asarkos*, and yet in context it clearly doesn't

15. McFarland, "Spirit and Incarnation," 149–53.
16. McFarland, "Spirit and Incarnation," 150.
17. Tanner, *Decrees*, 86.
18. Williams, *Arius*, 244.

reduce the existence of the Son to a temporal event, as though birth from Mary is also the originating event of the Trinity. Rather, Williams grounds the union of divinity and humanity in the hypostasis of the Word, the Word who is the "condition" of the human existence.[19] In this sense, *logos asarkos* seems to warrant both a "no" and, perhaps, a qualified "yes." No, there is no temporally pre-existent (or post-existent) Logos; no, we cannot identify the Son independently of Jesus's life. This is in no small part because event-plotting in God's life is impossible or, at minimum, liable to serious risks. But this incarnate life also seems uniquely and unsubstitutably held forward by God as the mode of divine power in the world, so that God's hypostatic identity (especially in the procession of God the Son) is known *in* that life and nowhere else.[20] God's eternal triune life seems nonetheless to be the hypostatic grounding of the human life, and in this limited sense, *logos asarkos* seems to have some use.[21]

What does this mean about the passibility or impassibility of the eternal Word? The one divine person, God the Son, is both impassible and passible without contradiction or a process or change from one to the other. By denying a temporally preexistent *logos asarkos*, the event of incarnation does not involve a transition on the Word's part, a new episode in the "biography of the Word," in which the Word goes from unenfleshed to enfleshed or from impassible to passible. Rather, Jesus is impassible *according to the divine nature* and passible *according to the human nature*. In both attributions, there is only one subject, one "who"—the eternal second hypostasis of the Trinity. How is this possible? In the incarnation, we are contemplating a complete

19. See also Williams, "Trinity and Ontology," 161.
20. Williams, *Christ the Heart*, 56.
21. Cf. McFarland, *Word Made Flesh*, 85–88.

union of full humanity and full divinity in one and the same person, without the natures becoming "confused" or "changed"—again, the kind of "impassibility" appropriate to God is true of Jesus (according to his divine nature), and the kind of passibility appropriate to humanity is true of Jesus (according to his human nature).[22] Even more: as Thomas Weinandy was quoted in an earlier chapter, "God is impassible precisely because he is *supremely passionate* and cannot become any more passionate."[23] This is the kind of "impassibility" appropriate to simplicity understood as "inclusive transcendence"—God is not simply the negation of "passion" or "change" (understood univocally) but is the overfullness of existence from which all passion and change are made possible.[24] The divine Son is by (divine) nature simple—the infinite actuality of *ipsum esse*—which means that the Son's eternal personhood is constituted divinely by an excess of passion compatible with the human passion lived in his human nature. Consequently, when the Son, who by nature simply *is* God, becomes human and lives and suffers humanly, no "change" or alternation of the divine *nature* takes place.[25] Again, this is because the Son's divine nature is an excess of passion, and so the Son can therefore embrace human passion in his own hypostasis. This is still an act of *kenosis* (Phil 2:7) but not in the sense of setting aside or divesting divine "properties"—rather, it is an act of personal identification with humble and obediential human life.[26]

22. Cf. Pawl, "Incarnation of a Simple God," 303–17.

23. Weinandy, *Does God Suffer?*, 126–27 (emphasis added).

24. So I'm sympathetic with Jenson's claim that, on the question of God's passibility, it's best to speak in negations, both "not impassible" and "impassible"; cf. Jenson, "*Ipse pater*," 93–101.

25. Cf. Riches, *Ecce Homo*, 197–204.

26. White, "Divine Perfection and Kenosis," 137–56.

ASYMMETRICAL CHRISTOLOGY AND THE ACTIVE HUMANITY OF JESUS CHRIST

This raises additional questions how the two natures of Christ are related: i.e., the communication of attributes (*communicatio idiomatum*). I've already said that all that is true of God is true of Jesus and that all that is true of his human life is true of one and the same Jesus. But do "properties" of the divine nature get attributed to Jesus's *humanity*? Or vice-versa? If it goes just one way, from the divine nature to the human nature, say, then the relationship is asymmetrical. In post-reformation scholasticism, the communication of attributes was distinguished into four kinds (see fig. 7.2): the *genus idiomaticum*, the *genus apostelesmaticum*, the *genus maiestaticum*, and the *genus tapeinoticum*. The first two follow from the discussion above and restate the conclusion that humanity and divinity remain unconfused, unaltered (*genus idiomaticum*), and inseparable (*genus apostelesmaticum*) in the hypostatic union. The third, according to which the human nature participates in divine properties, historically divided Lutheran scholastics, who affirmed it, from Reformed scholastics, who rejected it. And the fourth, in which the divine nature takes on properties of the human nature, was a hypothetical possibility rejected by most until recent years.[27]

---

27. Cf. Holmes, "Asymmetrical Assumption," 365–71.

PART II: EXPERIMENTS IN CHRISTIAN DOCTRINE

Fig. 7.2—*Communicatio idiomatum* (Communication of Attributes)		
genus idiomaticum	"the aspect of predication"	attributes of each nature are predicated of the one person
genus apostelesmaticum	"the aspect of mission"	the cooperation of humanity and divinity in all Jesus's action
genus maiestaticum	"the aspect of majesty"	participation of the human nature in divine attributes (e.g., eternity, omniscience, omnipresence)
genus tapeinoticum	"the aspect of humiliation"	participation of the divine nature in human attributes (e.g., suffering, mortality, divine alienation)

According to divine simplicity, is there a reason to prefer one over the other? In his 2018 book, *Christ the Heart of Creation*, Rowan Williams defends a broadly Thomistic Christology, grounded in a doctrine of God comparable to the one I'm developing here. At times, Williams seems to go beyond the simple point I attributed to him above—i.e., that the Logos is the "condition" of incarnation, but incarnation is not "an episode in the biography of the Word." Here, Williams argues that between the human and divine natures in Christ, there is a similar asymmetry as the one that obtains between God and creation:

> The Word is identified in principle quite independently of Jesus in the sense that nothing in human history makes the Word to be anything that the Word is not eternally . . . Yet a complete account of the Word and a consideration of how in fact the Word is made known in the world would need to refer to Jesus of Nazareth; . . . this emphatically does not mean that there is anything but a *wholly one-sided relation between Word and Jesus*. . . . The life of Jesus is not simply "the same thing as" the life of the Word, since it

is what it is *because of the inexhaustible action that pervades and structures it.*[28]

In context, Williams is drawing a careful parallel between the divine-human relation in Christ and the relationship between Jesus and the church. Through dialogue with Bonhoeffer, Williams wants to affirm the unique universal character of the church, while avoiding a triumphalist or Constantinian ecclesiology.[29] But what is striking is that the union of two natures in one hypostasis is being treated as an encompassing of one nature within the other (human within divine). This is the reverse of what I worried Jenson tended toward above. The asymmetry—namely, that the divine nature is unaffected by the human nature, but the human nature is pervaded and structured by the divine— seems appropriate, considering that God is *the creator* and so is the all-pervading and structuring source of finite being. This seems to permit, though Williams doesn't state it, a *genus maiestaticum*, the gift of divine properties to the human nature through the union. An asymmetrical Christology. However, two critiques have been raised against this approach.

First, Bruce McCormack argues that this kind of theology displays an internal tension, one that Chalcedonian Christology has never been able to overcome. Because the one divine hypostasis "pervades" and "structures" the human life, McCormack argues that the human nature tends to be construed as a receptive *instrument* of the Son's divine agency. This renders the humanity purely passive, and it teeters on the brink of Docetism, the idea that the Son play-acts as a human.[30] This is a serious concern. The problem is, in

28. Williams, *Christ the Heart*, 77 (emphasis added).

29. E.g., Williams, *Christ the Heart*, 199–217.

30. McCormack, *Humility*, 42–65.

McCormack's diagnosis, the direction of the asymmetrical active–receptive relation, which in Chalcedonian theology, and in Williams's above, seems to go exclusively from divinity to humanity. McCormack's solution is to maintain an asymmetry, but to invert its traditional orientation—God the Son is "receptive," and the human nature is "active."[31] The divine Son simply is the immutable relation of "ontological receptivity," eternally directed toward Jesus's human act of being.[32]

McCormack's proposal is rich and nuanced, forging a new path for Reformed theology (which also means that full assessment of his proposal ought to come from within that tradition, rather than my Wesleyan/Anglo-Catholic perspective). Most striking to me is his commitment to immutability while rejecting impassibility and simplicity, since impassibility is typically treated as a corollary of immutability. The core question for present purposes is whether McCormack's charge of human passivity follows for my account of simplicity, because if he's right, the result is Docetism. There are two reasons I don't think simplicity requires purely passive/receptive humanity in the incarnation. First, the question of divine simplicity is largely secondary in the grammar of the hypostatic union, since it is at the level of the *hypostasis* that the union takes place. The hypostasis *is* composed (in a sense), concretely "personalizing" both divinity and humanity. If divinity is "simple" in this union, that doesn't directly problematize the completeness of the

---

31. Cf. the final chapter for his Reformed "repair" of Chalcedon; McCormack, *Humility*, 253–70.

32. Cf. McCormack, *Humility*, 251–53. While this sounds like a rejection of the *genus maiestaticum* in favor of the *genus tapeinoticum*, McCormack insists that he "reject[s] the entire apparatus that produced it" (252).

humanity, because both humanity and divinity subsist in their respective entirety as the same person.

Second, McCormack assumes that "simplicity" depends on "substance metaphysics," which creates the problem for Christology of "two discreet [sic] (substantially conceived) 'natures' subsisting in one and the same 'person.'"[33] Whether or not McCormack's label of "substance metaphysics" has any validity, the purported problem he identifies *couldn't* obtain in my account: there simply cannot be *two discrete* natures, because the simple divine nature is infinite, inclusively transcendent, and unbounded. That is, the divine nature could never be "discrete" vis-à-vis any creaturely reality—God is "other" as the *not-other*.[34] Or: God is distinct as the non-discrete. The human nature certainly is discrete (in two ways), but neither diminishes the active reality of Jesus's humanity. (i) Human nature is "discrete" as finite, so that to say Jesus's human nature is "discrete" is just to say that he is spatiotemporally localized and contingent. (ii) Human nature is "discrete" by virtue of hypostasis, so that Jesus's human nature is discrete in just the same way any other human's is: by being concretized as that one hypostasis (in distinction from others). But to be discrete in this way is not to be rendered passive, rather, it's the condition of the possibility of being a particular, finite, human agency. At the level hypostasis, the Logos' divine nature is not discrete vis-à-vis the human nature, since both are identical to one and the same hypostasis. If Williams approach, for instance, uses this grammar to attribute *all* the action to divine agency (rather than, say, divine-human, or "theandric," agency), then he has gone further than the grammar itself requires. For if the hypostasis is the subject of action, and the hypostasis of Jesus is the union of

33. McCormack, *Humility*, 252.
34. Nicholas of Cusa, *God as Not-Other*.

humanity and divinity, then the action of Jesus is no less human than it is divine, whether divinity is simple or not. I don't see how inverting an asymmetrical relation accomplishes anything other than a repetition of the problem in the opposite direction. Finally, at this stage McCormack's proposal seems open to other christological problems, in particular a two subject Christology (Nestorianism).[35]

However, in his penetrating account of Maximus the Confessor's theology, Jordan Daniel Wood critiques the asymmetry itself, arguing that the hypostatic union is strictly symmetrical.[36] At the level of Christology, Wood's concerns seem comparable to the point I've been maintaining throughout this chapter: that the one hypostasis has two natures, and therefore neither nature is altered or confused through union with the other. As Wood puts it, a hypostasis is "a positive principle that individuates and particularizes and that is *utterly indifferent to* . . . the universal (nature) and particular (characteristics) in and of every real being."[37] That is, a hypostasis has no "natural content" and so is "indifferent" to the nature(s) it individuates. To say the hypostasis is "indifferent" is to say that in individuating and particularizing a nature, the hypostasis *concretizes* (and so in a sense "preserves") the entirety of that nature's content.[38] For this reason, both of Christ's natures, human and divine,

---

35. Cf. Coakley, "Humility," 261–65; and Irving, "Critical Assessment," esp. 160–61.

36. See Wood's critique of Williams in "Against Asymmetrical Christology." For his constructive proposals, see *Whole Mystery of Christ*, esp. 19–53, 195–204.

37. Wood, *Whole Mystery of Christ*, 24.

38. Wood, *Whole Mystery of Christ*, 30–33. Wood uses this "Christo-logic" to generalize for all creation so that all creation is fulfilled/deified by literally sharing in the hypostatic union. I'm not sure I would go this far, though the originality of Wood's vision is remarkable.

stand in the same relation to the hypostasis—or said differently, the one hypostasis of Jesus stands in the same relation to humanity (*homoousion*) and divinity (*homoousion*). The relation is symmetrical because the union is not a "natural union" but a "hypostatic union." When reading Williams's Christology, Wood takes issue, then, with Williams's appeals to a purely divine Logos whose action "pervades and structures" the human life of Jesus, because this way of speaking seems to slip from one *composite hypostasis* (Jesus, aka Logos) to *a composite nature* (or a compositional relation at the level of natures).[39] Wood seems to offer a more promising way forward, for his approach rightly critiques a Logos-driven asymmetry at the level of natures without overcorrecting by inverting the asymmetry. Wood's proposals allow us to do something like what McCormack proposes—reject "the entire apparatus that produced" asymmetries[40]—but without facile rejection of metaphysics.

The abiding question of this chapter has been whether simplicity creates problems for the incarnation, and this has taken two forms: the so-called *logos asarkos* with the impassible/passible dynamic, and the question of (a)symmetry between the two natures. In one sense, my argument has been that simplicity doesn't seem to create any unique difficulties, because in both cases the conceptual distinction between hypostasis and nature does the principal work. If the union is at the level of hypostasis—one personal subject who individuates and particularizes the two natures—then the natures *as* natures don't seem to be changed or confused.

---

39. Wood, "Against Asymmetrical Christology"; interpreting Maximus, Wood says, "A composed hypostasis, not a composed nature—this is Maximus' line" (*Whole Mystery of Christ*, 29).

40. McCormack, *Humility*, 252.

Consequently, claiming that the divinity of Christ is simple and, in a qualified sense, "impassible" doesn't compete with the claim that the hypostasis, the one Logos/Jesus, is an active and suffering human. It is still the second Person of the Trinity *who* suffers and acts as this human. And simplicity also does not force a Logos-driven asymmetry between the natures, whereby the human nature is purely receptive vis-à-vis the divine nature's activity. This is because in the hypostatic union, the two natures are better thought of as symmetrical in their relation to each other (it is true "both ways," we could say, that the natures are united in one hypostasis without change, without confusion, without division, without separation).

So, Jesus is active *as a human* exactly like any other human is. As human, he is a finite creature, and so is ontologically dependent on God as creator. But as human, he also possesses a finite *esse* by which he actively self-communicates and lives that particular human life (see ch. 5). The "who" of that life is the Logos, fully divine and fully human. What about Jesus's miracles, prophetic action, and resurrection? As McFarland argues, these features of Jesus's life are enabled the same way Israel's prophets performed miracles and acted as divine representatives, and the same way any other human will be resurrected and glorified: by the Spirit (Judg 13:25; Joel 2:28–29; Zech 4:6; Acts 1:8; Rom 8:11–17).[41] Jesus is Word made flesh, and so our "kin." But as our "theandric" kin, Jesus is also the one who bears our sanctified humanity, and so births us into regenerate life in God. That is, the one simple God becomes, in the Word, our mother.

---

41. McFarland, "Spirit and Incarnation," 153–58. This is part of what McFarland calls a "Chalcedonianism without Reserve" (cf. *Word Made Flesh*, 1–16).

QUESTIONS

1. Why is the distinction between hypostasis and nature so important for Christology?
2. Did the proposed solution to the impassible God undergoing human kenosis and passion succeed?
3. What kind of "symmetrical" incarnation did this chapter seem to conclude with? Why does that seem to work for simplicity?

8

ESCHATOLOGY

I am the fiery life of divine substance, I blaze above the beauty of the fields . . . I am concealed in things as fiery energy. They are ablaze through me, like the breath that ceaselessly enlivens the human being, or like the wind-tossed flame in a fire. . . . I have breathed life into everything, so that nothing by its nature may be mortal, for I am life.

—HILDEGARD OF BINGEN[1]

HILDEGARD WORKS WITH A classical scriptural theme of the purifying form of God's judgment, a theme that provokes both awesome hope and trepidation. In Malachi, the Lord's coming is portentous, "For he is like a refiner's fire . . . he will sit as a refiner and purifier of silver, and he will purify the descendants of Levi and refine them like gold and silver

---

1. Hildegard, *Book of Divine Works*, 1.1.2 (trans. from *Selected Writings*, 172).

until they present offerings to the Lord in righteousness" (Mal 3:2–3a). This fiery judgment becomes a messianic expectation in Daniel, where the fire is processional, streaming out from the very presence of the Ancient One (Dan 7:10; also Isa 66:15–19). If we combine these visions with Hildegard's, we get an image of God's eschatological action as the very same creative power by which God works in creatures, making them "ablaze" with life. And since God's fiery life is the molten core of all creation, nothing is finally "mortal" or confined to the duration and impermanence of an immanent principle of existence. The "fiery life of divine substance" is the condition of the possibility of eternal life.

But how does divine simplicity affect the form and content of Christian hope? If the ultimate good for creation is to be united with God, does it make a difference if God is thought of as "simple"? In this chapter, I consider three ways simplicity could contribute to the Christian doctrine of "last things." First, the concept of *theosis* or deification evokes a strong sense of participation *in* God as the final form of union with God. If God is simple, can we participate in God in a strong sense while remaining different than God, persisting in the integrity proper to our creaturely uniqueness? Or does participation in God end up making creatures absolutely identical to the simple, indivisible essence of God? Second, if there are two outcomes for creatures—beatitude and perdition—are these predetermined by God's election? If God is the simple, pure act of existence who creates all, aren't we required to imagine that God's judgment is unilateral and all-decisive? That is, does simplicity require double-predestination? Third and finally, what about universalism? Although a minority report throughout church history, some recent arguments for universalism appeal to the logic of simplicity. These are not all compatible with each other—especially double

THEOSIS

Theosis is a powerful account of the goal of union with God. Hildegard's fire-imagery captures the kind of relationship theosis articulates. If we think of fire in a more elemental framework—i.e., as though "fire" were a basic constitutive *energy* or dynamism underlying physical phenomena—then anything "hot" *receives* its heat by participating in the elemental reality of "fire." Or, take a simile Aquinas was fond of: a blacksmith places iron in a furnace, and the iron becomes hot with the very heat of the fire itself, so that it can be said to "participate" in the heat proper to the fire.[2] Theosis is analogous to this relationship, in that redeemed creatures come to receive something of the perfection and eternity proper only to God, and this is only possible by an intimate relationship.[3] God just *is* divine perfection and eternity (per simplicity), therefore creatures only receive these qualities through participation in God. This is radical intimacy, becoming "partakers of the divine nature" (2 Pet 1:4 NKJV; also 1 Pet 2:4–5). The language of "partakers" seems to imply that redeemed creatures become *part* of God, or become something God "has." But God *is* all that God has, so that if God "has" creatures in this intimate way, doesn't that reduce to a relationship of strict identity? And wouldn't that mean that creatures cease to exist altogether, being rather absorbed into the simple divine nature?

If this is the logical consequence of articulating simplicity and theosis together, it seems like we have to choose

2. Aquinas, *Power of God*, 3.7.
3. Cf. Irenaeus, *Against Heresies*, 3.19.1.

Eschatology

between them. The question is, does theosis entail such a compositional relationship between God and redeemed creatures? In other words, in affirming theosis, are we claiming either (i) that God becomes a part of creatures in their perfection or that (ii) creatures become parts of God? My argument here is that divine simplicity rules out both these options, and that this actually *enables* a thorough affirmation of theosis without risk of dissolving the creator-creature distinction.

First, if God is simple, then God cannot "enter into the composition of other things," Aquinas argues. That is, God's simplicity is incompatible with God becoming a part, since God's simplicity is beyond the domain of parthood. As Aquinas understands it, a "cause" can only become part of its effects if (1) it has the same specific form as its effects (so a human parent shares something of its human form with their progeny), if (2) the action is already of a composite reality (a human acting by their hand), or if (3) it is only partially in act (or mixed-act, partially actual and partially potential).[4] All of these are ruled out by simplicity, which says God doesn't have a form (excluding 1), is non-composite (excluding 2), and is pure act (excluding 3). In short, only things existing within the same order of being might enter into compositional relationships—namely, within the plane of finite, composite beings. But God is *not* a being among beings but rather the creative source of all beings, immediately active and present to all creatures in a unique mode (Deut 10:14–17; Ps 139; Jer 23:23–24; Acts 17:28; Heb 2:10).[5] Therefore God is not the kind of real-

4. Aquinas, *ST*, 1.3.8.

5. And, as Aquinas argues, God doesn't have a "real relation" to creatures. Precisely because of the immediacy of God's presence there is no basis for a "real relation" in Aquinas's technical sense (Aquinas, *ST*, 1.13.7). See Platter, "Jesus, Trinity, and Creation," 235–39.

ity that can enter into composition with finite, composite creatures. And so in theosis, God does not become a "part" of the redeemed creature.

Perhaps, second, creatures become instead "parts" of God through theosis. However, this assumes either that creatures "add" something to God or that creatures slice up the divine being so that they have a partial share in God. The first option doesn't work with simplicity since nothing can be "added to" or "taken from" God (Eccl 3:14)—and again this is not due to a generic rejection of "passibility" or "mutability" in God's case but is rather grounded in God's excess and superabundance (Jas 1:17; 1 John 1:5; also, Isa 9:2; Ps 89:15–16). We can also reject the idea that creatures take on a partial share in (a now-composite) God. Whether we're thinking of participating in God's "existence" according to creation *ex nihilo* or in God's glory in theosis, "participating in God" never means that creatures slice up the divine being and claim their own little parcel of divinity. Simplicity provides a straightforward reason, namely a simple God simply can't be parceled out. But there's also a reason from the side of the creature who receives existence and glorification—namely, that existence/glory is received in a manner proper to the creature itself.[6] Consequently, the creature's existence is the *actualization* of its own form, and the creature's perfection through theosis is the *glorification* of its own form by beholding God's eternal glory (Rom 8:11; 2 Cor 3:9–11, 16–18; 4:6, 16–18).[7]

If neither compositional relationship is possible in theosis, the worrying sequence above is ruled out—namely, that if redeemed creatures become "part" of God, and God is all God has, then "having" redeemed creatures entails

6. Aquinas, *ST*, 3.54.2; and *Power of God*, 3.3.

7. Aquinas, *ST*, 3.Suppl. 85.1; 3.Suppl. 92.1–2; Aquinas, *ScG*, 2.55.9–13. Cf. Davison, "Deification and Participation," 547–61.

Eschatology

that God and creatures become identical. In fact, the opposite seems to follow from the logic of divine simplicity. Because God is simple, creaturely intimacy never adds to God in a composition-like way, and God can be inexhaustibly intimate and inclusive of creatures without alteration or confusion in God's being. In theosis, creatures receive God's perfection, eternity, and glory in a manner proper to their creaturely mode of being, so that increasing intimacy with God by participation *intensifies and reaffirms* (i.e., perfects) the particularity of the glorified creature.[8]

DIVINE SIMPLICITY AND DOUBLE PREDESTINATION

There have been several opportunities in this book to draw on the biblical imagery of God as light, but of course light is contrasted with darkness. This raises the prospect of a fundamental duality: light versus dark (Isa 9:2; Ps 89:15–16; Mic 7:8; Jas 1:17), faith versus unbelief (John 1:9; 3:19–21; 8:12), obedience versus wickedness (Prov 4:18–19; 15:29–30; Eph 6:12), wisdom versus folly (Prov 13; Eccl 2:13). When 1 John says that "God is light, and in him there is no darkness at all" (1:5b), it articulates the opposition between lying or the spirit of antichrist on the one hand and God's love on the other (2:18–28). There is no getting around the fact that unbelief and wickedness are incompatible with the genuine fellowship of God's presence, and this seems to imply that some—perhaps many—will finally be excluded from fellowship with God (Matt 25:31–33, 46; Rev 20:10–15).[9]

---

8. Cyril of Alexandria, *Commentary of John*, 1.9: "When the Son is in a position, he is in it unchangeably. But we are placed into sonship, and we are gods by grace. We are not ignorant of what we are. This is the way in which we believe that the saints too are light" (p. 49). See also Aquinas, *ScG*, 3.19.1; 2.23.10.

9. Cf. Augustine, *Enchiridion*, 24.97.

If we accept for the moment the possibility of a dual-outcome—beatitude for the faithful and perdition for the unbelieving—then it is natural to ask on what basis God determines their fates. There seems to be two general options: either God judges based on persons' deeds (Matt 25:40–45; Rev 20:13) or God eternally predetermines according to God's inscrutable will (Rom 8:29–30; 9:16–24; Eph 1:3–10). Recognizing the dilemma of these scriptural precedents, John Calvin (1509–1564) draws on the logic of divine simplicity to develop his own solution.[10] It's crucial to recognize that Calvin's articulation of election is placed within his discussion of the Christian life, sanctification, and assurance. This is a testament to Calvin's attention to biblical context, where most New Testament discussions of election and predestination are addressed to believers' faltering confidence in the adequacy of their faith (e.g., Rom 8:24–39).[11]

When he considers the possibility that God's judgment is based on human deeds, he rules it out for two reasons. First, this would devolve into works righteousness, as though humans earn their ultimate fate. While that would accord with human sensibilities about justice, it doesn't adequately address the question of assurance where genuine self-knowledge more often reveals one's *inadequacy* and *lack of merit* before God (3.15.2). Second, this would put God's election at the whim of creaturely integrity, which would mitigate against the efficacy of God's electing promises and would make God's choice and redemptive work *dependent* upon creaturely states (3.24.1; 3.24.3).

---

10. Calvin, *Institutes*, 3.18; 3.21–24. Cited parenthetically for the remainder of this section.

11. We're dealing here with the "affective salience of doctrine": cf. Zahl, *Spirit and Experience*, 37–40. Consequently, assessment of Calvin's arguments would have different results if considered in a different context than descriptive eschatology.

Eschatology

This means that God's simple aseity rules out judgment based on merit in favor of strict predestination according to God's inscrutable will (3.23.5; 3.24.14).[12] God determines humanity to perdition not only as a just consequence for the demerit of unbelief, but God also directly determined humanity to fall altogether—a *decretum quidem horribile*, "indeed a horrifying decree" (3.23.7, alt.). Why must it be the case that humanity fell by God's decree rather than by their own free choice? Because "no one can deny that God foreknew what end man was to have before he created him, and consequently foreknew *because he so ordained by his decree*" (3.23.7; emphasis added). Calvin is committed to the idea that God is "simple," which is instrumental in all his trinitarian claims (e.g., 1.13.2; 1.13.4–5; 1.13.19–20; 1.13.22). And on the basis of simplicity, Calvin rules out the idea that anything happens without being directly foreknown and willed by God: "Nothing is more absurd than that anything should happen without God's ordaining it. . . God's will is the highest and first cause of all things because nothing happens except from his command" (1.16.8).[13] Again, it is foreknown *because* it is willed by God, and not vice-versa (3.23.7). This is reasonable according to divine simplicity: God is pure act and consequently doesn't "react" to creaturely events.

Altogether, this seems a strong case for taking double predestination (that God directly decrees both who is saved

---

12. Barth criticizes Calvinist appeals to God's inscrutable will, which invite the projection of a generic idea of pure will without any attention to the concrete form of God's choosing revealed in Jesus Christ. Cf. *CD*, II/2, esp. 44–76.

13. The original quotation includes "or permission," but in his doctrine of election he denies the legitimacy of distinguishing God's willing and permitting (3.23.8). Mullins's concerns about a "modal collapse" (discussed in ch. 6) might be valid for Calvin's understanding of the God-world relation.

and who is damned) as an entailment of divine simplicity. God's election is not *conditioned* by "foreknowledge," because (as simple) God is absolutely *unconditioned*.[14] Again, if it is the case that some persons will be redeemed and some damned, and that both are ordered to the glory of God, then God is the cause of both destinies. And as cause, God is not reactive to creaturely merits but is the precondition from eternity of these destinies. That is, God decrees, according to God's primordial act of will alone, the eternal destiny of every human—a double decree, because the decree directs to blessedness and to damnation.

While there is an internal coherence to Calvin's doctrine, it faces serious challenges. First, this view encounters difficulty with a variety of biblical texts. Contrary to Calvin's attempt to ground perdition exclusively in God's "inscrutable will," Lamentation says that "the Lord will not reject forever . . . for he *does not willingly afflict or grieve anyone*" (Lam 3:31, 33). In this light, it seems a category mistake to make God's act of rejection or condemnation a matter of *willing*, since it appears that God *doesn't* willingly do such things. Further, St. Paul himself, so often cited in support of double predestination (esp. Rom 8:29–30; 9:16–24; Eph 1:3–10), unqualifiedly affirms Christ's universal scope and inclusivity:

> The free gift is not like the trespass. For if the many died through the one man's trespass, much more surely have the grace of God and the gift in the grace of the one man, Jesus Christ, abounded for the many (Rom 5:15).

The free gift *is not like the trespass*—is this because the trespass has a stronger and more exhaustive reach than the free

---

14. See also Turretin, *Institutes*, 4.7.5–7; 4.9.19–20; 4.11.10–24; 4.17.21.

gift, so that it will claim more people or in any way defeat the free gift? This way of framing the disanalogy is contrary to the logic of this passage, where Paul doubles down on the universality of grace over-against condemnation: "Just as one man's trespass led to condemnation *for all humans*, so one man's act of righteousness leads to justification and life *for all humans*" (Rom 5:18, alt.; also 1 Cor 15:22).[15] The "universality" of condemnation and righteousness is not symmetrical or balanced, because grace abounds in excess of sin (Rom 5:20). Consequently, the disanalogy between the free gift and the trespass seems to consist in the greater reach of Christ's grace—that the universality of grace overtakes the universality of condemnation. Calvin and his epigones have responses to the questions these passages raise, though they strike me as exegetically unpersuasive (despite their popularity).[16]

Second, this view faces a serious problem with divine simplicity, which raises the specter of internal inconsistency. God's double decree is primordial, eternally preceding the individuals whose fate it seals. Both destinations

15. In both instances of "for all," the Greek is *eis pántas anthrṓpous*.

16. Calvin only cites Rom 5:18 in his discussion of Christology (once in the whole *Institutes*), far removed from the doctrine of election. Turretin, however, has an ingenious solution. The "all" in the case of Christ's gift of life is "taken here not distributively (for the individuals of classes) but collectively (for classes of individuals), i.e., as Beza renders it 'for all sorts' . . . In this sense, God wills not that all men individually, but some from every class or order of men should be saved" (Turretin, *Institutes*, 4.17.34). Turretin draws on the precedent of Augustine in addition to the cited Beza; cf. *Enchiridion*, 27.103. But why is Christ's justification and life only "for all" *collectively* while the condemnation because of Adam's trespass is "for all" *distributively*? This is at best question-begging and at worst directly contrary to the rhetorical force of Paul's statement, where the abounding excess of grace is unqualifiedly celebrated. Consider the exchange between Thomas Talbott and I. Howard Marshall in Parry and Partridge, *Universal Salvation?*, esp. 66–68, 251–54.

(beatitude and perdition) have God not only as cause but also as *telos*—both are ordered to divine glory, revealed as mercy (for the elect) and as justice (for the reprobate).[17] So, the dual outcome is grounded in God's eternal identity itself, which suggests that God's identity is irreconcilably dual.[18] This follows directly from Calvin's arguments that ground election and rejection in God's inscrutable will. God's double decree is not *based* on foreknowledge but is the precondition of foreknowledge, which means that God's double decree has only God's nature/will as its source. It was purportedly divine simplicity that required this conclusion, but now the conclusion removes the veil of divine simplicity to reveal a more fundamental divine duality. And even worse, because the divine duality grounds the opposing outcomes of beatitude and perdition, the duality in God seems to have a comparable ethical polarity: God is not only "good" (corresponding to the blessedness God bestows upon the elect) but also "evil" (corresponding to the misery God metes out on the damned).

DIVINE SIMPLICITY AND UNIVERSALISM

If a predestined dual outcome risks construing God as primordially dualistic, perhaps divine simplicity is more compatible with a single ultimate outcome: that all will finally be redeemed. Since Origen (and the anathemas against him at the Second Council of Constantinople in 553 CE), universalism has been known by the Greek term *apokatastasis*, typically meaning something like "restoration to original condition." This word and its corresponding verb can be found in both the Septuagint (the Greek translation of the Hebrew Bible) and the New Testament (e.g., Job 5:18; Jer

17. E.g., Calvin, *Institutes*, 3.23.8; 3.25.5.
18. My critique here is inspired by Hart, *All Shall Be Saved*, 90.

15:19; Ezek 16:55; Matt 17:11; Mark 9:12; Acts 3:21).[19] There is some tension in Scripture on the issue of universal salvation, as noted above. Thomas Talbott suggests that there are three eschatological claims in Scripture that cannot coherently be held together without significantly qualifying or rejecting at least one of them. They could be put this way:

1. God desires the redemption of every person (1 Tim 2:4, 4:10; 2 Pet 3:9; Lam 3:22, 3:31–3).

2. Nothing can defeat God's redemptive action, so everyone God wants to redeem will be redeemed (Eph 1:11; 1 Cor 15:27–8; Col 1:20; Rom 5:18).

3. Some persons will not be redeemed and will consequently be separated from God eternally (Matt 25:46; Eph 5:5; 2 Thess 1:9).[20]

Clearly one can affirm 1 and 2 *or* affirm 2 and 3, but not all three together without qualification. If God desires the redemption of everyone (1), and God's redemptive desires cannot be defeated (2), then everyone will be redeemed (contra 3). But if nothing can defeat God's redemptive desires (2), and not all will be redeemed (3), then God desires the redemption of only some and not all (contra 1).

There are a variety of ways one might uphold a plain reading of the third claim without altogether rejecting the first. The readiest approach would be to qualify the claim that God desires the redemption of every person, rather than outrightly rejecting it.[21] But in this section, I'm con-

19. Cf. Ramelli, *Larger Hope?*, 1:1–19.

20. Cf. Talbott, *Inescapable Love of God*, 37–40. The wording is my own paraphrase. McClymond, *Devil's Redemption*, 950–52, misconstrues these propositions as a "philosophical argument" for universalism, taking them out of their preparatory context as though Talbott thinks they produce a universalist conclusion on their own (which they obviously don't).

21. Again, see Turretin, *Institutes*, 4.17.34; also n16 above.

sidering how simplicity might be invoked to articulate the indefeasible universality of God's redemptive activity (1 and 2), which instead requires qualifying the third claim on the "eternality" of separation from God.[22] One immediate clue for connecting simplicity and universalism might be discovered in Scripture, "[God] desires *everyone to be saved and to come to the knowledge of the truth. For there is one God*" (1 Tim 2:4–5a). The singularity of God's desire (the salvation of everyone) is grounded in the singularity and unity of God. And if divine simplicity is not taken univocally as a kind of brute uniformity or opposition to variation but as inclusive transcendence, then the simplicity of God is compatible with various forms of creaturely flourishing (see ch. 6). Consequently, the singular desire of the simple God (salvation of all) can include diverse creatures without collapsing them into a monolithic unity or a preordained dual outcome.

Grounding the effects of God's redemptive activity in the being of God in this way sets the contrast between light and dark in a different frame. God's light is not a static reality, set in a Manichaean eternal opposition to darkness.[23] Rather: "God is light, and in him there is no darkness at all"

22. Universalists argue that the New Testament term *aiṓnion*, translated as "eternal" for "eternal punishment," doesn't mean everlasting in the way our English word "eternal" suggests (for that, Greek usually used *aïdios*); cf. Ramelli, *Larger Hope?*, 1:215–21; and Hart, *New Testament*, 537–44. So, for instance, when Matt 25:41 says some must depart "into the eternal fire" (*eis tò pūr tò aiṓnion*), this doesn't mean that they will burn everlastingly, but that the fire is of "another age" or lasts "a long time." The fire would, then, denote a temporary purification rather than an eternal (everlasting) punishment.

23. In his early anti-Manichaean polemics, Augustine sounds universalist: "the goodness of God . . . disposes *all things* that fall away so that they occupy the place most suited to them *until, by an ordered movement, they return to that from which they fell away*" (*Catholic and Manichaean*, 2.7.9; emphasis added).

Eschatology

(1 John 1:5b; also, Isa 9:2; Ps 89:15–16; Mic 7:8). And James says, "Every good gift and every perfect gift is from above, and comes down from the Father of lights, with whom there is no variation or shadow of turning" (1:17 NKJV). So "darkness" (e.g., unbelief, disobedience, human condemnation, etc.) is not a function of God's "decree" or something that has any claim to coeternity with God, because God is light with *no* "shadow of turning." That is, God is *simply* light.

Rather than containing shadow or retributive intent, God's light is manifest for therapeutic and healing ends (Titus 2:11–13). When Scripture identifies God with light, its focus is often on the life of discipleship for which God is both means and end. In one of the Johannine "I am" sayings, Jesus says, "I am the light of the world. Whoever follows me will never walk in darkness but will have the light of life" (John 8:12; compare 1:9). The theme of "walking in the divine light" reaches eschatological climax in Revelation 21, where God's glory is the sole illumination in the new Jerusalem (21:23). The walls and streets of the city are "pure gold, *transparent as glass*" (21:18, 21), so that the divine light is placed within the new Jerusalem and unobstructed by the city's walls. God's light becomes a gravitational center drawing to itself "the glory and the honor of all nations" (21:26; also Isa 66:20–23). Darkness is not equiprimordial with divine light but is that which God's light eschatologically overcomes. It is the unbelief that could never "overtake" the light of Christ (John 1:5; 3:17–21), because the light of Christ will finally "enlighten everyone" (John 1:9). That is, with the *appearance* of God's grace (in Christ), God brings "salvation to all humans" (Titus 2:11, alt.).

For many early church theologians, the therapeutic light of God introduces an ethical aspect to eschatology.[24] One can only live in the light—discipleship and faith—if

---

24. Cf. Ramelli, *Larger Hope?*, 1:*passim*; summary at 1:211.

one has a proper vision of the light—the gift of grace. So, is it appropriate for God to condemn those whose failure to believe or to lead a good life is a function of an obstructed vision of the light of Christ? It doesn't seem right to hold someone morally accountable for their unbelief independent of the requisite vision of the source and object of belief (Num 22:22–34). Consequently, eschatology is the horizon of God's pedagogy, preparing *all* for a genuine vision of the light itself in whom alone one can see (Ps 36:9; Heb 8:11) and of the Good through whom all good is enacted (Ps 16:2; Mark 10:18; Jas 1:17). According to divine simplicity, God is the good-itself without admixture of any contrary (light with no "shadow of turning"). The *telos* of all moral action and formation is the good-itself, which is nothing other than God. Humans fail in their pursuit of goodness only by misidentifying the good, thereby falling short of their intrinsic *telos*.[25] However, if God's action is a pedagogy of the good (the "Good" that, again, names the entirety of God), then anytime a creature's moral development is arrested, God's pedagogy is thwarted or defeated. Universalists and double-predestinarians agree that nothing can defeat God's pedagogy (or redemptive desires). But according to universalism, God's redemptive desire is nothing other than God's own goodness with no admixture of its opposite, so that the redemptive desire that cannot be defeated is that God's goodness be known and participated by all—that God *be* "all in all" (1 Cor 15:28; cf. Rom 11:32).[26]

Along these lines, David Bentley Hart argues that universalism is entailed by the moral character of the God

---

25. Cf. Gregory of Nyssa, *Death and Eternal Life*, 65–85, on the eschatological primacy of the Good; and *Soul and Resurrection*, 71–73, 77–79, 85, on the pedagogical purification of the soul.

26. Cf. Parry, *Larger Hope?*, 2:7.

who creates *ex nihilo*.²⁷ Hart understands God's creative act to be a teleologically ordered act, so that the "end" is in the beginning and the end displays God's moral and metaphysical character. If God is simple, God's whole creative act receives its integrity from its orientation to the singular end of God's creative act—namely, beatitude, i.e. communion with God. To deny that God's creative act is ordered to a singular end manifesting the simple goodness of the creator is, Hart argues, to deny that God creates *ex nihilo*.²⁸ The postulate of any other final end for creatures would require an additional force or being outside God's creation, and this force or being could not be God's creation (since if it were, it too would be ordered ultimately to God's singular end). In other words, Hart argues that a non-universalist eschatology is also a non-monotheistic theology, for only if there are opposing divine beings could there be opposing outcomes for creation. It seems, then, that if the outcome of creation's history is a function of God's moral character, then all will ultimately be restored (*apokatastasis*). God's simple goodness cannot but bring all things to fruition in divine fellowship.

While this strikes me as more coherent than the double predestinarian theology, it is not without difficulties.²⁹ First, this eschatology seems focused on redemption of sinners according to their guilty status. This raises the question of whether universalism is an eschatology for oppressors, designed to relinquish guilt for actively perpetrating evils or to distract from complicity in oppressive

27. Hart, *All Shall Be Saved*, Part II, First Meditation.

28. Hart, *All Shall Be Saved*, 67–73.

29. Aside from the two I discuss, consider McClymond, *Devil's Redemption*, 125–55, 246–78 (concerns about gnostic influences), 445–568, 1004–13 (concerns about divine dualism) and 1013–33 (concerns about grace).

structures.[30] In this light, universalism can appear as a kind of theodicy—an attempt to *justify* the presence of evil in light of the goodness of God. However, this oppressor position sits uncomfortably with the context of many scriptural accounts of divine judgment, where God is the only one who can liberate the oppressed from the horrors perpetrated against them.[31] Would universalism still be plausible were one to center social and systemic evils and the experience of victims rather than perpetrators?

This leads to the second difficulty, which intersects more directly with divine simplicity. Universalism risks speculating more directly and cataphatically about God's eschatological judgment than seems appropriate, especially in light of the mystery of both God and suffering.[32] Certainly, theology ought to think carefully about how any eschatological vision comports with other claims about God and creation.[33] But the certainty with which some universalists assert the necessity of a particular kind of postmortem reconciliation seems to read off a set of entailments too directly from claims about God, especially considering the apophatic character of our knowledge of a simple God. As Kathryn Tanner argues, "links of presupposition and implication" from our concept of God are "highly fragile."[34] If universalism is treated as a direct entailment of divine simplicity, it may distort the apophatic and analogical way in which God is identified as simple.

---

30. Cf. Cone, *Black Theology and Black Power*, 121–27; Cone, *Black Theology of Liberation*, 144–51; and Evans, *We Have Been Believers*, 172–81.

31. Cf. Cone, *God of the Oppressed*, 57–76.

32. Cf. Kilby, "Eschatology, Suffering, and Limits," 285–91; and McFarland, *Hope of Glory*, 83–109.

33. Cone, *Black Theology of Liberation*, 150–51.

34. Tanner, "*Ex Nihilo*," 140, also 138–40.

Eschatology

If we follow Hildegard's connection of divine fire and purification unto eternal life, eschatology cannot be separated from an articulation of God's infinite, simple being. On theosis, I argued that simplicity actually helps mitigate against the dissolution of the distinction between God and creation. But in the remainder of the chapter, the results have been more mixed. I sampled two controversial approaches to eschatological judgment—double predestination and universalism—showing how each relies on the logic of divine simplicity to secure their eschatological conclusions. Both approaches encounter challenges, whether on scriptural or systematic-theological grounds. Certainly, universalism fared better in my account than double predestination, but both seem overly confident in their speculations about postmortem judgment and its outcome. However, this exercise has demonstrated the relevance of divine simplicity for eschatology. It aids in affirming theosis without compromising creaturely integrity, and it has value for critically engaging controversial proposals in eschatology, both to understand their logic and to assess their potential.

QUESTIONS

1. This chapter used Aquinas's argument that God cannot enter into composition to argue that divine simplicity ensures that theosis doesn't result in creatures being absorbed without remainder. Did this argument succeed? What additional questions need to be addressed?

2. This chapter argued that in the end, double predestination compromises the doctrine of divine simplicity,

leading to incoherence. Can you restate that argument? How might Calvin respond?

3. What are two challenges to universalism, and what role does simplicity play? How could someone defend universalism in response?

CONCLUSION

God Whose Giving Knows No Ending

THROUGHOUT THIS BOOK, I'VE offered an invitation to the doctrine of divine simplicity. At one level, this has taken the form of introducing key distinctions, concepts, and historical precedents for the doctrine. But at another level, I have offered my own synthesis to present one way divine simplicity might contribute to a unified theological vision. That synthesis has at its core a spiritual vision, a sense that "doctrine" articulates a lived engagement with the utterly unique reality of God. For this reason, I have resisted a merely "scholastic" description of God's inner being, even though I don't assume a post-Kantian epistemology for which God's inner life is a sequestered noumenal reality to which access is strictly barred.

The heart of my account of divine simplicity could be captured in two claims. The first is that talk about God involves "persisting in asking unanswerable questions." This first appeared as a "what" question that situates divine simplicity in an apophatic context, since the what question is unanswerable and so sets limits for God-talk. But it also integrates the necessity of lived practices, since it's a question we *persist* in asking precisely because it's unanswerable but concerns the very meaning of God. In this light, I suggested that "metaphysical" language is appropriate within certain constraints. By focusing on the idea of "God" from within the vocation of love (1 John 4), I grounded "metaphysical" description in God's inclusive transcendence. That is, God is known through love of creaturely neighbors—in particular through loving the love by which we love creaturely neighbors, which means loving *God* in and through love of neighbor. Consequently, the descriptive terms we use to know and address other creatures can be used analogically for God, insofar as God is known and loved in (and beyond) other creatures.

This leads to the second core claim: "describing" God is a doxological act of *naming*. Divine names, following Dionysius, are ways of praising the entirety of God in response to the procession of God in and through creaturely realities. The divine names tradition also provides a bridge from the unanswerable but livable "what" question (of the simple "divine nature") to the unanswerable but livable "who" question (of the Holy Trinity). Here God's intrinsically processional life—the triune life—comes into focus. This triune life is what we live into and are bound to in our doxological naming of God. To speak about the Holy Trinity is to praise the very ground of our being and life.

Simplicity is about the processional life of God, known by God's procession in and through creation (infinite reality proceeding throughout finite reality) and eternally existing in triune perichoretic procession. To say that God's life is "processional" is to say that God exists as gift. But what does it mean for God to give? In the perspective of simplicity, it means that God withholds nothing, because God cannot be divided into the given and the reserved. And yet, in every divine gift, the entirety of God is given in excess of what any creature can receive. So, God is given without reserve, refracted according to the finite mode proper to creaturely recipients of the divine gift, and therefore known now in a glass darkly (1 Cor 13:12). According to divine simplicity, then, we can say that God gives without reserve *and* that God's "giving knows no ending."[1]

I hope this overview might invite further exploration of divine simplicity. And I recognize that the book might just as well confirm the inadequacy of simplicity for some readers. In that case, perhaps it at least helps to understand some of the historic reasons divine simplicity has been taken seriously and how it might inflect other doctrines in both traditional and novel ways. In that lens, it could still enrich dialogue where there's often impasse. Though I've aimed to provide an accurate and attractive account of God as simple, the final tests will be the value it brings to actual life with God and the extent to which it aids in understanding and engaging constructively with long-standing theological teachings. But Underhill's claim is the primary goal: the "art of union with Reality," with "life at its most intense point."[2] If God's simplicity is another term for God's inclusive transcendence, then intimacy with God is also a radically open and self-giving act of intimacy with reality-itself, with the present realities given to us to love. All reality is gift, because all reality is embraced in the God whose giving knows no ending. The God who is

1. Edwards, "Hymn #678."
2. Underhill, *Practical Mysticism*, 3; Underhill, *Mysticism*, 29.

the infinite and eternal gift-exchange of Triune Life. The God who overflows in self-donation from irrepressible plenitude and thereby invokes finite witness and participation—the simple, triune God.

BIBLIOGRAPHY

Abraham, William J. *Divine Agency and Divine Action*. 4 vols. New York: Oxford University Press, 2018–2021.

Adams, Robert Merrihew. *Finite and Infinite Goods: A Framework for Ethics*. New York: Oxford University Press, 1999.

Adler, Amitai. "What's in a Name?: Reflections Upon Divine Names and the Attraction of God to Israel." *Jewish Bible Quarterly* 37 (2009) 265–69.

Anatolios, Khaled. *Retrieving Nicaea: The Development and Meaning of Trinitarian Doctrine*. Grand Rapids: Baker Academic, 2011.

Anselm. *The Major Works*. Edited by Brian Davies and G. R. Evans. New York: Oxford University Press, 1998.

———. "Prayer to St. Paul." In *The Prayers and Meditations of Saint Anselm, with the Proslogoion*, translated by Sister Benedicta Ward, 141–56. London: Penguin, 1973.

Aquinas, Thomas. *Commentary on The Metaphysics*. Translated by John P. Rowan. Latin/English Edition of the Works of St. Thomas Aquinas 50–51. Green Bay, WI: Aquinas Institute, 2020. https://aquinas.cc/la/en/~Metaph.

———. *Disputed Questions on the Power of God*. Translated by Shapcote, Lawrence. Latin/English Edition of the Works of St. Thomas Aquinas 25. Green Bay, WI: Aquinas Institute, 2023. https://aquinas.cc/la/en/~QDePot.

———. *On Being and Essence*, in *Opuscula I: Treatises*. Latin/English Edition of the Works of St. Thomas Aquinas 55. Green Bay, WI: Aquinas Institute, 2018. https://aquinas.cc/la/en/~DeEnte.

———. *Summa Contra Gentiles*. Translated by Lawrence Shapcote. Latin/English Edition of the Works of St. Thomas Aquinas 11–

12. Green Bay, WI: Aquinas Institute, 2019. https://aquinas.cc/la/en/~SCG1.

———. *Summa Theologiae*. Translated by Lawrence Shapcote. Latin/English Edition of the Works of St. Thomas Aquinas 13–20. Green Bay, WI: Aquinas Institute, 2012. https://aquinas.cc/la/en/~ST.I.

Aristotle. *Metaphysics*. Translated by Hugh Lawson-Tancred. London: Penguin, 1998.

———. *Posterior Analytics*. Edited and translated by Jonathan Barnes. Revised Oxford Translation. The Complete Works of Aristotle. Princeton: Princeton University Press, 1991.

Ashworth, E. Jennifer, and Domenic D'Ettore. "Medieval Theories of Analogy." In *The Stanford Encyclopedia of Philosophy*, edited by Edward N. Zalta, 2021. https://plato.stanford.edu/archives/win2021/entries/analogy-medieval.

Augustine. *The Catholic and Manichaean Ways of Life*. Translated by Donald A. Gallagher and Idella J. Gallagher. Washington, DC: Catholic University of America Press, 1966.

———. *The City of God*. 2 vols. Translated by William Babcock. The Works of Saint Augustine: A Translation for the 21st Century. New York: New City, 2013.

———. *Enchiridion on Faith, Hope, and Love*. Translated by Bruce Harbet. In *On Christian Belief*, edited by Boniface Ramsey, 273–343. The Works of Saint Augustine: A Translation for the 21st Century. Hyde Park, NY: New City, 2005.

———. *Tractates on the Gospel of John 112–24 and Tractates on the First Epistle of John*. Translated by John W. Rettig. Washington, DC: Catholic University of America Press, 1995.

———. *The Trinity*. Translated by Edmund Hill. The Works of Saint Augustine: A Translation for the 21st Century. Hyde Park, NY: New City, 1991.

Baker-Fletcher, Karen. *Dancing with God: The Trinity from a Womanist Perspective*. St. Louis: Chalice, 2006.

Balthasar, Hans Urs von. *Love Alone is Credible*. Translated by D. C. Schindler. San Francisco: Ignatius, 2004.

———. *Presence and Thought: An Essay on the Religious Philosophy of Gregory of Nyssa*. Translated by Mark Sebanc. San Francisco: Ignatius, 1995.

Barnes, Michel René. "De Régnon Reconsidered." *Augustinian Studies* 26 (1995) 51–79.

Barrett, Jordan P. *Divine Simplicity: A Biblical and Trinitarian Account*. Minneapolis: Fortress, 2017.

Bibliography

Barth, Karl. *Church Dogmatics I/1–IV/4*. Edited by Geoffrey W. Bromiley and T. F. Torrance. Edinburgh: T. & T. Clark, 1956–1975.

———. *The Epistle to the Romans*. Translated by Edwyn Clement Hoskyns. 2nd ed. London: Oxford University Press, 1933.

Basil the Great. *On Christian Doctrine and Practice*. Translated by Mark DelCogliano. Yonkers, NY: St. Vladimir's Seminary Press, 2012.

Bauckham, Richard. *The Bible and Ecology: Discovering the Community of Creation*. Waco, TX: Baylor University Press, 2010.

Bauerschmidt, Frederick Christian. *The Love that Is God: An Invitation to Christian Faith*. Grand Rapids: Eerdmans, 2020.

Behr, John. *John the Theologian and His Paschal Gospel: A Prologue to Theology*. Oxford: Oxford University Press, 2019.

Black, C. Clifton. "First, Second, and Third Letters of John." In *The New Interpreter's Bible Commentary*, edited by Leander E. Keck, 12:363–469. Nashville: Abingdon, 1998.

Bohmbach, Karla G. "Names and Naming in the Biblical World." In *Women in Scripture: A Dictionary of the Named and Unnamed Women in the Hebrew Bible, the Apocryphal/Deuterocanonical Books, and the New Testament*, edited by Carol Meyers, 33–39. Boston: Houghton Mifflin, 2000.

Brower, Jeffrey E. "Making Sense of Divine Simplicity." *Faith and Philosophy* 25 (2008) 3–30.

Burrell, David B. *Aquinas: God and Action*. Edited by Mary Budde Ragan. 3rd ed. Eugene, OR: Wipf & Stock, 2016.

———. *Knowing the Unknowable God: Ibn-Sina, Maimonides, Aquinas*. Notre Dame: University of Notre Dame Press, 1986.

Butner, D. Glenn, Jr. "For and Against de Régnon: Trinitarianism East and West." *International Journal of Systematic Theology* 17 (2015) 399–412.

———. *Trinitarian Dogmatics: Exploring the Grammar of the Christian Doctrine of God*. Grand Rapids: Baker Academic, 2022.

Calvin, John. *Institutes of the Christian Religion*. Edited by John T. McNeill. Translated by Ford Lewis Battles. Repr. Louisville, KY: Westminster John Knox, 2006.

Chesterton, G. K. *St. Thomas Aquinas*. London: Hodder & Stoughton, 1933. https://ccel.org/ccel/chesterton/aquinas/aquinas.i.html.

Childs, Brevard S. *The Book of Exodus: A Critical, Theological Commentary*. Louisville, KY: Westminster John Knox, 1974.

Clarke, W. Norris. *Explorations in Metaphysics: Being—God—Person*. Notre Dame: University of Notre Dame Press, 1994.

Bibliography

Cleveland, Christena. *God is a Black Woman*. New York: HarperCollins, 2022.

Coakley, Sarah. *God, Sexuality, and the Self: An Essay "On the Trinity."* Cambridge: Cambridge University Press, 2013.

———. "The Humility of the Eternal Son." In *Christology Revised: Keuz, Auferweckung, Menschwerdung, "Jesus Remembered,"* edited by Heinrich Assel and Bruce L. McCormack, 259–68. Berlin: Walter de Gruyter, 2024.

———. *The New Asceticism: Sexuality, Gender, and the Quest for God*. New York: Bloomsbury, 2015.

———. "'Persons' in the 'Social' Doctrine of the Trinity: Current Analytic Discussion and 'Cappadocian' Theology." In *Powers and Submissions: Spirituality, Philosophy, and Gender*, 109–29. New York: Blackwell, 2002.

Coffey, David. *Deus Trinitas: The Doctrine of the Triune God*. Oxford: Oxford University Press, 1999.

Cone, James H. *Black Theology and Black Power*. Repr. Maryknoll, NY: Orbis, 1997.

———. *A Black Theology of Liberation*. 40th Anniversary. Repr. Maryknoll, NY: Orbis, 2010.

———. *God of the Oppressed*. Rev. ed. Maryknoll, NY: Orbis, 1997.

Crisp, Oliver D. "A Parsimonious Model of Divine Simplicity." *Modern Theology* 35 (2019) 558–73.

Cyril of Alexandria. *Commentary of John*. Translated by David R. Maxwell and Joel C. Elowsky. Ancient Christian Texts 1. Downers Grove, IL: IVP Academic, 2013.

Davison, Andrew. "Deification and the Metaphysics of Participation." In *The Oxford Handbook of Deification*, edited by Paul Gavrilyuk et al., 547–61. New York: Oxford University Press, 2024.

———. *Participation in God: A Study in Christian Doctrine and Metaphysics*. Cambridge: Cambridge University Press, 2019.

De Haan, Daniel. "Thomist Classical Theism: Divine Simplicity Within Aquinas' *Triplex Via Theology*." In *Classical Theism: New Essays on the Metaphysics of God*, edited by Jonathan Fuqua and Robert C. Koons, 101–22. New York: Routledge, 2023.

Dionysius the Areopagite. *The Celestial Hierarchy*. In *The Complete Works*, translated by Colm Luibheid, 143–91. Mahwah, NJ: Paulist, 1987.

———. *The Divine Names*. In *The Complete Works*, translated by Colm Luibheid, 47–131. Mahwah, NJ: Paulist, 1987.

Dolezal, James E. *God Without Parts: Divine Simplicity and the Metaphysics of God's Absoluteness*. Eugene, OR: Pickwick, 2011.

Duby, Steven J. *Divine Simplicity: A Dogmatic Account*. London: Bloomsbury T. & T. Clark, 2016.

Duns Scotus, John. *Questions on Aristotle's Categories*. Translated by Lloyd A. Newton. Washington, DC: Catholic University of America Press, 2014.

Edwards, Robert L. "Hymn #678: God, Whose Giving Knows No Ending." In *Evangelical Lutheran Worship*. Repr. Hymn Society, 2006.

Emery, Gilles. *The Trinitarian Theology of Saint Thomas Aquinas*. Translated by Francesca Aran Murphy. Oxford: Oxford University Press, 2007.

Evans, James H., Jr. *We Have Been Believers: An African American Systematic Theology*. Edited by Stephen G. Ray Jr. 2nd ed. Minneapolis: Fortress, 2012.

Farrer, Austin. *Finite and Infinite: A Philosophical Essay*. Westminster: Dacre, 1943.

Frege, Gottlob. "Dialogue with Pünjer over Existence." In *Posthumous Writings*, edited by P. Long and R. White, 53–67. Oxford: Blackwell, 1979.

Fretheim, Terence E. *Exodus: A Bible Commentary for Teaching and Preaching*. Louisville, KY: John Knox, 1991.

Gilson, Etienne. *God and Philosophy*. New Haven: Yale Nota Bene, 1954.

Gorman, Michael J. *Cruciformity: Paul's Narrative Spirituality of the Cross*. Grand Rapids: Eerdmans, 2001.

———. *Inhabiting the Cruciform God: Kenosis, Justification, and Theosis in Paul's Narrative Soteriology*. Grand Rapids: Eerdmans, 2009.

Green, David Gordon, dir. *Dickinson*. Season 1, episode 2, "I Have Never Seen 'Volcanoes.'" Aired November 1, 2019, on Apple TV+.

Gregory of Nazianzus. *On God and Christ: The Five Theological Orations and Two Letters to Cledonius*. Translated by Frederick Williams and Lionel Wickham. Crestwood: St. Vladimir's Seminary Press, 2002.

Gregory of Nyssa. *Contra Eunomium I-III*. Translated by Stuart George Hall. 3 vols. Leiden: Brill, 2007–2018.

———. "Homily 7." In *Homilies on Ecclesiastes*, edited by Stuart George Hall, translated by Stuart George Hall and Rachel Moriarty, 111–27 Berlin: Walter de Gruyter, 1993.

———. *On Death and Eternal Life*. Translated by Brian E. Daley. Popular Patristics. Yonkers, NY: St. Vladimir's Seminary Press, 2022.

———. "On 'Not Three Gods:' To Ablabius." In *Nicene and Post-Nicene Fathers of the Christian Church, Second Series*, edited by Philip Schaff and Henry Wace, translated by William Moore and Henry Austin Wilson, 5:331–36. Edinburgh: T. & T. Clark, 1892.

———. *On the Soul and the Resurrection*. Translated by Catherine P. Roth. Crestwood: St. Vladimir's Seminary Press, 1993.

Griffiths, Paul J. *Intellectual Appetite: A Theological Grammar*. Washington, DC: Catholic University of America Press, 2009.

Gunton, Colin E. "Eastern and Western Trinities: Being and Person. T. F. Torrance's 'Doctrine of God.'" In *Father, Son, and Holy Spirit: Toward a Fully Trinitarian Theology*, 32–57. New York: T. & T. Clark, 2003.

———. *The One, the Three, and the Many: God, Creation and the Culture of Modernity*. Cambridge: Cambridge University Press, 1993.

Hart, David Bentley. *The Beauty of the Infinite: On the Aesthetics of Christian Truth*. Grand Rapids: Eerdmans, 2003.

———. *The Experience of God: Being, Consciousness, Bliss*. New Haven: Yale University Press, 2013.

———. *The New Testament: A Translation*. 2nd ed. New Haven: Yale University Press, 2023.

———. *That All Shall Be Saved: Heaven, Hell, and Universal Salvation*. New Haven: Yale University Press, 2019.

Hauerwas, Stanley. *With the Grain of the Universe: The Church's Witness and Natural Theology*. Grand Rapids: Baker Academic, 2001.

Hector, Kevin W. *Christianity as a Way of Life: A Systematic Theology*. New Haven: Yale University Press, 2023.

Hilary of Poitiers. *On the Trinity*. Edited by Philip Schaff and Henry Wace. Translated by S. D. F. Salmond. Nicene and Post-Nicene Fathers of the Christian Church Second Series 9. Edinburgh: T. & T. Clark, 1899.

Hildegard of Bingen. *Book of Divine Works: With Letters and Songs*. Edited by Fox. Sante Fe, NM: Bear and Co, 1987.

———. "O Viriditas Digiti Dei." International Society of Hildegard von Bingen Studies (blog), July 5, 2022. https://www.hildegard-society.org/2022/07/o-viriditas-digiti-dei-responsory.html.

———. *Scivias*. Translated by Columba Hart and Jane Bishop. New York: Paulist, 1990.

———. *Selected Writings*. Translated by Mark Atherton. New York: Penguin, 2001.

Hinlicky, Paul R. *Divine Simplicity: Christ the Crisis of Metaphysics*. Grand Rapids: Baker Academic, 2016.

Bibliography

Holmes, Stephen R. "Asymmetrical Assumption: Why Lutheran Christology Does Not Lead to Kenoticism or Divine Passibility." *Scottish Journal of Theology* 72 (2019) 357–74.

Idol Killer. "Divine Simplicity Is True—Ortlund vs Mullins— Debate Openings." YouTube, April 12, 2024. https://youtu.be/LrvXXL4md3A?si=TH-YniI3hXi6a2My.

Irenaeus. *Against Heresies*. Edited by Alexander Roberts and James Donaldson. Ante-Nicene Fathers of the Church 1. Edinburgh: T. & T. Clark, 1885.

Irving, Alex. "A Critical Assessment of Bruce L. McCormack's Christological Proposal." *Scottish Journal of Theology* 77 (2024) 149–62.

Jenson, Robert W. "*Ipse Pater Non Est Impassibilis*." In *Theology as Revisionary Metaphysics: Essays on God and Creation*, edited by Stephen John Wright, 93–101. Eugene, OR: Cascade, 2014.

———. "Once More on the *Logos Asarkos*." In *Theology as Revisionary Metaphysics: Essays on God and Creation*, edited by Stephen John Wright, 119–24. Eugene, OR: Cascade, 2014.

———. *Story and Promise: A Brief Theology of the Gospel About Jesus*. Philadelphia: Fortress, 1973.

———. *Systematic Theology*. 2 vols. Oxford: Oxford University Press, 1997–1999.

———. *The Triune Identity: God According to the Gospel*. Philadelphia: Fortress, 1982.

John of Damascus. *An Exact Exposition of the Orthodox Faith*. Edited by Philip Schaff and Henry Wace. Translated by S. D. F. Salmond. Nicene and Post-Nicene Fathers of the Christian Church, Second Series 9. Edinburgh: T. & T. Clark, 1899.

Julian of Norwich. *Revelations of Divine Love*. Translated by Barry Windeatt. Oxford: Oxford University Press, 2015.

Jüngel, Eberhard. *God as the Mystery of the World: On the Foundation of the Theology of the Crucified One in the Dispute between Theism and Atheism*. Translated by Darrell L. Guder. Grand Rapids: Eerdmans, 1983.

———. *God's Being is in Becoming: The Trinitarian Being of God in the Theology of Karl Barth*. Translated by John Webster. 2nd ed. Edinburgh: T. & T. Clark, 2001.

Keller, Catherine. *On the Mystery: Discerning Divinity in Process*. Minneapolis: Fortress, 2008.

Kerr, Fergus. *Theology After Wittgenstein*. 2nd ed. London: SPCK, 1997.

Bibliography

Kilby, Karen. "Eschatology, Suffering, and the Limits of Theology." In *Game Over?: Reconsidering Eschatology*, edited by Christophe Chalamet et al., 179–91. Berlin: Walter de Gruyter, 2017.

Knauer, Peter. *Der Glaube kommt vom Hören: Ökumenische Fundamentaltheologie*. 6th ed. Freiburg: Herder, 1991.

LaCocque, André. "The Revelation of Revelations." In *Thinking Biblically: Exegetical and Hermeneutical Studies*, by André LaCocque and Paul Ricoeur, 307–29. Translated by David Pellauer. Chicago: University of Chicago Press, 1998.

Lacugna, Catherine Mowry. *God for Us: The Trinity and Christian Life*. New York: HarperCollins, 1991.

Lampassi, Giovani, dir. *Brooklyn Nine-Nine*. Season 6, episode 1, "Honeymoon." Aired January 10, 2019, on NBC.

Leithart, Peter J. *Creator: A Theological Interpretation of Genesis 1*. Downers Grove, IL: IVP Academic, 2023.

———. "What Sorts of Parts Is God Without?" Theopolis Institute (blog), July 25, 2019. https://theopolisinstitute.com/conversations/what-sorts-of-parts-is-god-without/.

Lieu, Judith M. *I, II, and III John: A Commentary*. New Testament Library. Louisville, KY: Westminster John Knox, 2008.

Lindbeck, George A. *The Nature of Doctrine: Religion and Theology in a Postliberal Age*. 25th Anniversary Edition. Louisville, KY: Westminster John Knox, 2009.

Locke, John. *An Essay Concerning Human Understanding*. Edited by Peter H. Nidditch. New York: Oxford University Press, 1975.

Long, D. Stephen. *The Perfectly Simple Triune God: Aquinas and His Legacy*. Minneapolis: Fortress, 2016.

Louth, Andrew. *Denys the Areopagite*. New York: Continuum, 1989.

Loux, Michael J., ed. *The Possible and the Actual: Readings in the Metaphysics of Modality*. Ithaca: Cornell University Press, 1979.

Maimonides, Moses. *The Guide for the Perplexed*. Translated by M. Friedländer. Second Revised Edition. Skokie, IL: Varda, 2002.

Mann, William E. "Divine Simplicity." *Religious Studies* 18 (1982) 451–71.

Marion, Jean-Luc. *God Without Being: Hors-Texte*. Translated by Thomas A. Carlson. 2nd ed. Chicago: University of Chicago Press, 2012.

Marshall, Bruce D. *Trinity and Truth*. Cambridge: Cambridge University Press, 2000.

———. "The Unity of the Triune God: Reviving an Ancient Question." *Thomist* 74 (2010) 1–32.

Marshall, I. Howard. *The Epistles of John.* New International Commentary on the New Testament. Grand Rapids: Eerdmans, 1978.

Mascall, E. L. *Existence and Analogy: A Sequel to "He Who Is."* London: Longmans, Green, 1949.

Maximus the Confessor. "Difficulty 10." In *Maximus the Confessor,* edited and translated by Andrew Louth, 91–152. New York: Routledge, 1996.

———. *On the Cosmic Mystery of Jesus Christ.* Translated by Paul M. Blowers and Robert Louis Wilken. Crestwood: St. Vladimir's Seminary Press, 2003.

McClymond, Michael J. *The Devil's Redemption: A New History and Interpretation of Christian Universalism.* 2 vols. Grand Rapids: Baker Academic, 2018.

McCormack, Bruce L. *The Humility of the Eternal Son: Reformed Kenoticism and the Repair of Chalcedon.* New York: Cambridge University Press, 2021.

McFague, Sallie. *The Body of God: An Ecological Theology.* Minneapolis: Fortress, 1993.

McFarland, Ian A. *From Nothing: A Theology of Creation.* Louisville, KY: Westminster John Knox, 2014.

———. "'God, the Father Almighty': A Theological Excursus." *International Journal of Systematic Theology* 18 (2016) 259–73.

———. *The Hope of Glory: A Theology of Redemption.* Louisville, KY: Westminster John Knox, 2024.

———. "Spirit and Incarnation: Toward a Pneumatic Chalcedonianism." *International Journal of Systematic Theology* 16 (2014) 143–58.

———. *The Word Made Flesh: A Theology of the Incarnation.* Louisville, KY: Westminster John Knox, 2019.

Migne, Jacques-Paul, ed. *Patrologiae Cursus Completus, Series Graeca Prior, in qua Prodeunt Patres, Doctores Scriptoresque Ecclesiae Graecae.* 161 vols. Petit-Montrouge, 1857–1866. http://graeca.patristica.net/.

———, ed. *Patrologiae Cursus Completus, Serie Prima et Secunda, in quae Prodeunt Patres, Doctores Scriptoresque Ecclesiae Latinae a Tertulliano ad Innocentium III.* 217 vols. Petit-Montrouge, 1841–1855. http://latina.patristica.net/.

Miller, Barry. *The Fullness of Being: A New Paradigm for Existence.* Notre Dame: University of Notre Dame Press, 2002.

Moberly, R. W. L. *The God of the Old Testament: Encountering the Divine in Christian Scripture.* Grand Rapids: Baker Academic, 2020.

Moltmann, Jürgen. *The Trinity and the Kingdom: The Doctrine of God*. Translated by Margaret Kohl. London: SCM, 1981.

Mullins, R. T. *The End of the Timeless God*. New York: Oxford University Press, 2016.

———. "Simply Impossible: A Case against Divine Simplicity." *Journal of Reformed Theology* 7 (2013) 181–203.

Mullins, R. T., and Shannon Eugene Byrd. "Divine Simplicity and Modal Collapse: A Persistent Problem." *European Journal for Philosophy of Religion* 14 (2022) 21–51.

Murphy, Francesca Aran. *God Is Not a Story: Realism Revisited*. Oxford: Oxford University Press, 2007.

Nicholas of Cusa. *On God as Not-Other: A Translation and an Appraisal of* De Li Non Aliud. Translated by Jasper Hopkins. 3rd ed. Minneapolis: Arthur J. Banning, 1987.

———. "On Learned Ignorance." In *Nicholas of Cusa: Selected Spiritual Writings*, translated by H. Lawrence Bond, 85–206. New York: Paulist, 1997.

Oakes, Edward T. *Pattern of Redemption: The Theology of Hans Urs von Balthasar*. New York: Continuum, 1997.

Oliver, Simon. *Creation: A Guide for the Perplexed*. London: Bloomsbury T. & T. Clark, 2017.

O'Rourke, Fran. *Pseudo-Dionysius and the Metaphysics of Aquinas*. Notre Dame: University of Notre Dame Press, 1992.

Parry, Robin A. *A Larger Hope?*, vol. 2: *Universal Salvation from the Reformation to the Nineteenth Century*. Eugene, OR: Cascade, 2019.

Parry, Robin A., and Christopher H. Partridge, eds. *Universal Salvation?: The Current Debate*. Grand Rapids: Eerdmans, 2004.

Pawl, Tim. "The Incarnation of a Simple God." In *Classical Theism: New Essays on the Metaphysics of God*, edited by Jonathan Fuqua and Robert C. Koons, 303–17. New York: Routledge, 2023.

Perl, Eric D. *Thinking Being: Introduction to Metaphysics in the Classical Tradition*. Leiden: Brill, 2014.

Placher, William C. *The Domestication of Transcendence: How Modern Thinking about God Went Wrong*. Louisville, KY: Westminster John Knox, 1996.

Plantinga, Alvin. *Does God Have a Nature?* Milwaukee: Marquette University Press, 1980.

Plantinga, Cornelius, Jr. "Gregory of Nyssa and the Social Analogy of the Trinity." *The Thomist* 50 (1986) 325–52.

———. "Social Trinity and Tritheism." In *Trinity, Incarnation, and Atonement: Philosophical and Theological Essay*, edited by

Ronald J. Feenstra and Cornelius Plantinga Jr., 21–47. Notre Dame: University of Notre Dame Press, 1990.

Plato. *Parmenides*. Translated by Harold North Fowler. Loeb Classical Library 167. Cambridge, MA: Harvard University Press, 1926.

———. *Phaedo*. Translated by Christopher Emlyn-Jones and William Preddy. Loeb Classical Library 36. Cambridge: Harvard University Press, 2017.

Platter, Jonathan M. "Divine Simplicity and Scripture: A Theological Reading of Exodus 3:14." *Scottish Journal of Theology* 73 (2020) 295–306.

———. *Divine Simplicity and the Triune Identity: A Critical Dialogue with the Theological Metaphysics of Robert W. Jenson*. Berlin: Walter de Gruyter, 2021.

———. "Jesus, Trinity, and Creation: Divine Simplicity, the 'Real' Relation, and Trinitarian Economy in Dialogue with Robert Jenson." *Pro Ecclesia* 28 (2019) 233–52.

Radde-Gallwitz, Andrew. *Basil of Caesarea, Gregory of Nyssa, and the Transformation of Divine Simplicity*. Oxford: Oxford University Press, 2009.

Rahner, Karl. *The Trinity*. Translated by Joseph Donceel. New York: Crossroad, 1997.

Ramelli, Ilaria E. *A Larger Hope?* Vol. 1: *Universal Salvation from Christian Beginnings to Julian of Norwich*. Eugene, OR: Cascade, 2019.

Reiner, Rob. *The Princess Bride*. 1987. 20th Century Fox.

Riches, Aaron. *Ecce Homo: On the Divine Unity of Christ*. Grand Rapids: Eerdmans, 2016.

Roberts, Alexander, and James Donaldson, eds. *Ante-Nicene Fathers: The Writings of the Fathers Down to AD 325*. Edinburgh: T. & T. Clark, 1867. https://www.ccel.org/fathers.

Rocca, Gregory P. *Speaking the Incomprehensible God: Thomas Aquinas on the Interplay of Positive and Negative Theology*. Washington, DC: Catholic University of America Press, 2004.

Sammon, Brendan Thomas. *The God Who Is Beauty: Beauty as a Divine Name in Thomas Aquinas and Dionysius the Areopagite*. Eugene, OR: Pickwick, 2013.

Saner, Andrea D. *"Too Much to Grasp": Exodus 3:13–15 and the Reality of God*. Winona Lake, IN: Eisenbrauns, 2015.

Schaff, Philip, and Henry Wace, eds. *Nicene and Post-Nicene Fathers*, Second Series. Edinburgh: T. & T. Clark, 1886–1900. https://www.ccel.org/fathers.

Schärtl, Thomas. "Einfachheit Gottes und die Trinität." In *Eigenschaften Gottes: Ein Gespräch zwischen systematischer Theologie und analytischer Philosophie*, edited by Thomas Marschler and Thomas Schärtl, 379–409. Münster: Aschendorff Verlag, 2016.

Schwab, V. E. *The Invisible Life of Addie LaRue*. New York: Tor, 2020.

Schwöbel, Christoph. "Die Trinitätslehre Als Rahmentheorie Des Christlichen Glaubens: Vier Thesen Zur Bedeutung Der Trinität in Der Christlichen Dogmatik." In *Gott in Beziehung: Studien Zur Dogmatik*, 25–51. Tübingen: Mohr Siebeck, 2002.

Smith, Barry D. *The Oneness and Simplicity of God*. Eugene, OR: Pickwick, 2014.

Sonderegger, Katherine. *Systematic Theology*. 2 vols. Minneapolis: Fortress, 2015–2020.

Soskice, Janet Martin. *The Kindness of God: Metaphor, Gender, and Religious Language*. Oxford: Oxford University Press, 2007.

———. "Naming God: A Study in Faith and Reason." In *Reason and the Reasons of Faith*, edited by Paul J. Griffiths and Reinhard Hütter, 241–54. London: T. & T. Clark, 2005.

———. *Naming God: Addressing the Divine in Philosophy, Theology, and Scripture*. New York: Cambridge University Press, 2023.

Soulen, R. Kendall. *The Divine Name(s) and the Holy Trinity*. Vol. 1: *Distinguishing the Voices*. Louisville, KY: Westminster John Knox, 2011.

Spitzer, Robert J. *New Proofs for the Existence of God: Contributions of Contemporary Physics and Philosophy*. Grand Rapids: Eerdmans, 2010.

Stump, Eleonore. *Aquinas*. Arguments of the Philosophers. New York: Routledge, 2003.

Stump, Eleonore, and Norman Kretzmann. "Absolute Simplicity." *Faith and Philosophy* 2 (1985) 353–82.

Talbott, Thomas. *The Inescapable Love of God*. 2nd ed. Eugene, OR: Cascade, 2014.

Tanner, Kathryn. "Creation *Ex Nihilo* as Mixed Metaphor." *Modern Theology* 29 (2013) 138–55.

———. *God and Creation in Christian Theology: Tyranny or Empowerment?* Oxford: Basil Blackwell, 1988.

Tanner, Norman P. *Decrees of the Ecumenical Councils*. 2 vols. Washington, DC: Georgetown University Press, 1990.

Ticciati, Susannah. *A New Apophaticism: Augustine and the Redemption of Signs*. Leiden: Brill, 2013.

Bibliography

Tomaszewski, Christopher. "Collapsing the Modal Collapse Argument: On an Invalid Argument Against Divine Simplicity." *Analysis* 79 (2019) 275–84.

———. "How the Absolutely Simple Creator Escapes a Modal Collapse." In *Classical Theism: New Essays on the Metaphysics of God*, edited by Jonathan Fuqua and Robert C. Koons, 233–51. New York: Routledge, 2023.

Tonstad, Linn Marie. *God and Difference: Trinity, Sexuality, and the Transformation of Finitude*. London: Routledge, 2016.

Torrance, Thomas F. *The Christian Doctrine of God: One Being, Three Persons*. 2nd ed. Repr. London: Bloomsbury T. & T. Clark, 2016.

Trible, Phyllis. *God and the Rhetoric of Sexuality*. Philadelphia: Fortress, 1978.

———. *Texts of Terror: Literary-Feminist Readings of Biblical Narratives*. Philadelphia: Fortress, 1984.

Turretin, Francis. *Institutes of Elenctic Theology*. Edited by James T. Dennison Jr. Translated by George Musgrave Giger. 3 vols. Phillipsburg: P&R, 1992–1997.

Underhill, Evelyn. *Mysticism: A Study in the Nature and Development of Man's Spiritual Consciousness*. 12th ed. New York: Methuen, 1930. https://ccel.org/ccel/underhill/mysticism/mysticism.i.html.

———. *Practical Mysticism: A Little Book for Normal People*. New York: E. P. Dutton, 1914. https://ccel.org/ccel/underhill/practical/practical.ii.html.

Vallicella, William F. "Divine Simplicity: A New Defense." *Faith and Philosophy* 9 (1992) 508–25.

Velde, Rudi te. *Aquinas on God: The "Divine Science" of the Summa Theologiae*. Aldershot: Ashgate, 2006.

Wallace, David Foster. "This Is Water: Commencement Speech." Kenyon College, 2005. https://www.youtube.com/watch?v=DCbGM4mqEVw.

Weinandy, Thomas. *Does God Suffer?* Notre Dame: University of Notre Dame Press, 2000.

Wesley, John. *The Bicentennial Edition of the Works of John Wesley*. Vol. 13: *Doctrinal and Controversial Treatises II*. Edited by Paul Wesley Chilcote and Kenneth J. Collins. Nashville: Abingdon, 2013.

———. *A Plain Account of Christian Perfection*. Edited by Randy L. Maddox and Paul W. Chilcote. Kansas City: Beacon Hill, 2015.

———. *The Works of John Wesley*. 14 vols. Edited by Thomas Jackson. 3rd ed. Repr. Kansas City: Beacon Hill, 1978. https://wesley.nnu.edu/john-wesley/.

Bibliography

Wesley, John, and Charles Wesley. *Hymns and Sacred Poems (1740)*. The Poetical Works of John and Charles Wesley. London: Strahan, 1740. https://ccel.org/ccel/wesley/works/works.vii.html.

White, Thomas Joseph. "Divine Perfection and the Kenosis of the Son." In *Kenosis: The Self-Emptying of Christ in Scripture and Theology*, edited by Paul T. Nimmo and Keith L. Johnson, 137–56. Grand Rapids: Eerdmans, 2022.

Williams, Delores. *Sisters in the Wilderness: The Challenge of Womanist God-Talk*. Maryknoll, NY: Orbis Books, 1993.

Williams, Rowan. *Arius: Heresy and Tradition*. Rev. ed. Grand Rapids: Eerdmans, 2002.

———. *Christ the Heart of Creation*. London: Bloomsbury Continuum, 2018.

———. "Trinity and Ontology." In *On Christian Theology*, 148–66. Oxford: Blackwell, 2000.

Wittgenstein, Ludwig. *Philosophical Investigations*. Translated by G. E. M. Anscombe. Oxford: Blackwell, 2001.

Wolterstorff, Nicholas. "Divine Simplicity." *Philosophical Perspectives* 5 (1991) 531–52.

Wood, Jordan Daniel. "Against Asymmetrical Christology: A Critical Review of Rowan Williams's 'Christ the Heart of Creation.'" Eclectic Orthodoxy (blog), August 5, 2019. https://afkimel.wordpress.com/2019/08/04/against-asymmetrical-christology-a-critical-review-of-rowan-williamss-christ-the-heart-of-creation/.

———. *The Whole Mystery of Christ: Creation as Incarnation in Maximus the Confessor*. South Bend: University of Notre Dame Press, 2022.

Yarbrough, Robert W. *1–3 John*. Baker Exegetical Commentary on the New Testament. Grand Rapids: Baker Academic, 2008.

Zahl, Simeon. *The Holy Spirit and Christian Experience*. New York: Oxford University Press, 2020.

GENERAL INDEX

actuality and potentiality distinction, 37
actus purus (pure act), 37–38, 71, 81–82, 98, 101–4, 114, 121, 123, 141, 145
Adam and Eve, 50–52
Adams, Robert, 29, 32
analogia entis (analogy of being), 28, 36–37, 64–66, 70, 107
analogy, 26, 42, 60–64, 86–87, 154
  pros hen analogy, 26, 62–64, 87
Anselm, xxi, 107, 118n2
apokatastasis. *See* universalism
apophaticism, 5–6, 15, 24–25, 43, 50–51, 57–59, 61, 64, 73, 77–78, 90–91, 108, 154
aseity, 40, 47, 103, 145
Augustine, 5, 75, 76–78, 83–88, 95–96, 147n16, 150n23

Baker-Fletcher, Karen, 101n5
Barth, Karl, 6, 8–9, 74, 122, 145n12
Basil of Caesarea, 15

Bauckham, Richard, 113n30
Bonhoeffer, Dietrich, 131
Brooklyn Nine-Nine, 4, 11
Burrell, David, 8, 18–21, 47, 60

Calvin, John, 144–48
cheap grace, 115n33
Chesterton, G. K., xvii
Christ. *See* Jesus Christ.
christology, 88. *See also* Jesus Christ
  asymmetrical, 119–20, 129–35
  and Chalcedon, 120–21, 126
  communicatio idiomatum (communication of idioms), 119, 129–31
  and divine names, 57–59, 87–89
  heresies, 120–21, 124–26, 131
  hypostatic union, 120–21, 126–28, 135
Clarke, W. Norris, 110–11
Cleveland, Christena, 101, 115n34
Coakley, Sarah, xviii

General Index

Coffey, David, 79
creation, 60–61, 63–66, 107–16
    and creaturely submission, 80–82, 99–102
    and double agency, 106–13
    ex nihilo, 101, 107–8, 142, 152–53
    and modal collapse, 102–6, 112–15
Cyril of Alexandria, 143n8

Davison, Andrew, 114–15
de Régnon thesis, 74, 82
Dickinson, Emily, 100–102, 104, 114–15
"the distinction," 10, 20–21, 39
divine attributes, 40–41, 53–54, 56. *See also* divine names
divine gift, xxi, 12, 39, 67, 90–91, 110, 158–60
divine names, 34, 50–59, 65, 66–70, 83, 86–88, 95–97, 108, 152, 158. *See also* christology and divine names

economic Trinity. *See* Trinity, immanent and economic
eschatology, 80. *See also* predestination; universalism
esse (act of existence), 36, 40, 60, 67, 107–11, 114
essence and existence distinction, 9, 20–21, 38–39
equivocity, 26
existence. *See* metaphysics of existence

Farrer, Austin, 108–9
foreknowledge, 145–46. *See also* predestination
futurist ontology, 80, 124–25. *See also* simplicity, protological

Gorman, Michael J., 87
grammatical theology, 8, 13–17, 18–19, 41–44
    critique of, 24–25
    See also postliberalism; simplicity as grammar
Gregory of Nazianzus, 78n12, 88–89
Gregory of Nyssa, 15, 45, 76–78, 152n25
Griffiths, Paul, 102–3n9
Gunton, Colin, 75–77

Hagar, 51–52, 55, 66, 69
Hart, David Bentley, 39, 65, 150n22, 152–53
Hildegard of Bingen, xviii, 5, 13, 46–48, 49, 71, 73, 87, 138–39, 155
Hinlicky, Paul, 21n21
hypostasis (person), 120–21, 134

idolatry, 50–51. *See also* simplicity and idolatry
immanent Trinity. *See* Trinity, immanent and economic
immutability, 40, 43–44, 119, 121, 125, 132
impassibility, 38, 119, 127–28, 136
inclusive transcendence. *See* transcendence as non-contrastive / inclusive

incomprehensibility. *See* apophaticism
ineffability. *See* apophaticism
intensive definition, 29, 32, 54
ipsum esse (being-itself), 35–37, 67–70, 99, 121, 128
Irenaeus of Lyons, 14

Jenson, Robert, 6n5, 80–81, 101–2, 122–27
Jesus Christ, 57–60, 84, 86–88, 122–28, 146, 151–52
 as Mother, 117–18, 136
 See also christology; Logos (Word)
John of Damascus, 108–9
Julian of Norwich, xviii, 3, 23, 99, 117–18
Jüngel, Eberhard, 80–81, 101–2

kenosis, 86–87, 115n33, 119, 128
Keller, Catherine, 101n5

Lacugna, Catherine Mowry, 80
Leithart, Peter, 62n34, 94n49
Lindbeck, George, 16–17
Locke, John, 54
Logos (Word), 57, 59, 122–23
 logos asarkos (Word without flesh), 88, 122, 126–27
Long, D. Stephen, 94n49
love
 as Christian vocation, 29–32, 83–84, 86–87, 116, 158
 of God and neighbor, 31–33, 83–86, 143
 as participation, 32–33, 58, 85–88, 116, 159–60
 See also simplicity and love; Trinity and love

Mary. *See* Theotokos (Mary)
Maximus the Confessor, 57–60, 84n26, 88, 134
 on *logos/logoi*, 58–59, 114
McClymond, Michael, 149n20, 153n29
McCormack, Bruce L., 119–20, 125n14, 131–34
McFarland, Ian A., 59, 107–8, 125n14, 126, 136
metaphysics
 defined, 25
 of existence, 27–28, 36, 60, 110–11
 and God, 26–27, 35–36, 47, 59
 as the light, 151–52
 natures, 28–29
 one and many, 32–33
 and the transcendentals, 34–35
Miller, Barry, 26
Moberly, R. W. L., 67
Moltmann, Jürgen, 80–81, 101–2
Moses, 45, 66–70, 72
Mullins, R. T., 93, 95–97, 102–6, 108, 145n13
Murphy, Francesca Aran, 102

names/naming, 49–52. *See also* divine names
Nicholas of Cusa, 133
non-contrastive transcendence. *See* transcendence as non-contrastive / inclusive

177

Oakes, Edward, 65
omnipotence, 40
Origen, 148
ostensive definition, 29, 32, 54, 85

participation, xx, 10, 31, 33, 60–70, 85–87, 113–16, 140, 159–60. *See also* love as participation; theosis; Trinity and participation
perichoresis. *See* Trinity, perichoresis
Philo of Alexandria, 45
Plantinga, Alvin, 53–54
postliberalism, 17–20. *See also* grammatical theology; simplicity as grammar
predestination, 139–40, 143–48
    criticisms, 146–48
    vs merit, 144
    and permission, 145
prayer, 46–47
Princess Bride, The (movie), 83n21
Pseudo-Dionysius the Areopagite, 55–57, 66, 83, 88, 158

Rahner, Karl, 74–76. *See also* Trinity, Rahner's Rule
Ramelli, Ilaria E., 150n22
revelation, 41, 50, 57–59, 78
Rocca, Gregory, 61

salvation
    as being-made-simple, 117–18
Sammon, Brendan, 55, 69
Schwab, V. E., 49–50

Schwöbel, Christoph, 74–75, 92
Scotus, John Duns, 62
Septuagint, 148
simplicity
    and agnosticism, 24–25, 27, 61–62
    as apophatic claim, 5–6, 15, 19–21, 60, 73, 80, 157–58
    defined, xvii, 5, 61
    and doxology, 47–48, 60, 66, 69–70, 71–72, 158–59
    entailments, 40–41
    and light, 88–90, 143, 150–52
    and love, 28, 30–34, 83–85, 116, 159
    and final causation, 63–64, 68–70, 85–88, 111–15, 148, 152–53
    as grammar, 11, 18–21, 47, 71
    and the identity of essence and existence, 9, 38–40, 71, 104
    and the identity thesis, 40–41, 53–57
    and idolatry, 11, 18–21, 44, 66
    and metaphysics, 9–11, 27–41, 55–59, 63–66, 71
    and modal collapse, 102–6, 112–15
    and potentiality, 37–38, 102–3, 123
    protological, 80–81, 82, 102, 106–7, 115–16, 124–25
    Rahner's Rule, 79–82, 88n36, 101

and relationality, 92–95,
    141n5
and the sea of being, 108–10
and theological language,
    xx, 40–42, 47–48,
    53–56, 60–64, 95–97
and the transcendentals,
    34–35, 63–64
and Trinity, xvii–xviii, 44,
    74–77, 80–81, 89–92,
    95–98
Smith, Barry, 61n31
Social Trinity. *See* Trinity,
    Social Trinity.
Sonderegger, Katherine, 74,
    82n19
Soskice, Janet Martin, 54, 70, 118
Soulen, R. Kendall, 87

Talbott, Thomas, 149
Tanner, Kathryn, 39, 101n6,
    154
theodicy, 154
theosis, 139–43
Theotokos (Mary), 122–24
Thomas Aquinas, xvii, xviii,
    6–11, 33–36, 56, 62–
    64, 71, 83n20, 110n23,
    112–14, 140–42
  on existence. *See* esse
  on form, 114
  the "five ways," 7–8, 112n28
  on God and metaphysics,
    26n6
  and grammatical
    Thomism, 18, 20–21
  on the Trinity, 90n42,
    91n45, 94, 96
  on the *triplex via*, 44–45
Tomaszewski, Christopher,
    105–6

Tonstad, Linn Marie, 89–91
Torrance, T. F., 79
transcendentals. *See*
    metaphysics and
    the transcendentals;
    simplicity and the
    transcendentals
transcendence, 10, 31–33, 47,
    90, 141
  as "deep power," 115n34
  as non-contrastive /
    inclusive, 31–33, 39,
    64–65, 85, 93–95, 97,
    114, 116, 128, 133, 143,
    150, 159–60
transitivity of identity, 93, 96
Trible, Phyllis, 52, 69
Trinity
  and gender, 89–90
  immanent and economic,
    78–82
  and light, 88–92
  and love, 85–88
  and Nicaea, 77
  and participation, 83–88,
    92, 159–60
  perichoresis, 97, 158
  and predication, 95–97
  and processions, 85–86,
    88–92, 97–98, 126, 139,
    158–560
  psychological analogy,
    76–77
  and relations of origin, 90
  Social Trinity, 76–78
  subsistent relations, 90–92,
    95–96, 123–24
  and the trinitarian revival,
    74–79
  See also divine gift;
    simplicity and Trinity

179

triplex via, 24n2, 45, 47, 56, 71, 94–95, 97, 109–10. *See also* Thomas Aquinas on the *triplex via*
Turretin, Francis, 147n16

Underhill, Evelyn, xix, 74, 159
universalism, 139–40, 148–55
    criticisms, 153–54
    and God's redemptive desire, 146–47, 149–50, 152
    and meaning of "eternal," 150n22
univocity, 26, 42–44, 62, 69, 128

Wesley, Charles, 87
Wesley, John, 87, 110
Weinandy, Thomas, 38, 128
Williams, Rowan, 122, 126–27, 130–33, 135
Wittgenstein, Ludwig, 16–17, 112n28
Wolterstorff, Nicholas, 53
Wood, Jordan Daniel, 57n24, 119, 134–35
Word. *See* Logos (Word)

Zahl, Simeon, 144n11

SCRIPTURE INDEX

OLD TESTAMENT

Genesis
1:4	45
1:20–25	110
1:26–28	113
1:31	45
1:31—2:3	111
2:19–20	50
3:20	50
16:1–14	51–52
16:6	52
16:7–12	52
16:11	52
16:13	52

Exodus
3	45
3:1–12	68n48
3:6	68n48
3:13–16	50
3:13	68
3:14	35, 66–70
3:15–16	66
3:15	68
20:21	45
33	45
33:13—34:9	70
33:20	10

Numbers
22:22–34	152

Deuteronomy
6:4–5	30, 31n17
6:5	31
10:14–17	141
12:5	51
12:11	51
12:21	51

Judges
13:25	136

2 Samuel
22:2–3	66

1 Chronicles
5:11–26	45

Scripture Index

Job

5:18	148
26:14	10
38:1—40:2	51

Psalms

16:1–4	45
16:1–2	45
16:2	152
19:1–4	113
19:2–4	111
22:6	66
23:5–6	45
36:6–7	109
36:9	90, 152
65	56
89:15–16	142, 143, 150–51
99:3	50
100:5	45
104	66, 113
104:24–33	59
104:27–30	111
105:3–5	50
119:64–68	45
139	141
145:3	10
148	111, 113

Proverbs

4:18–19	143
8:22–36	111
13	143
15:29–30	143
16	111
16:31	114
16:33	111

Ecclesiastes

2:13	143
2:18–26	111
3:14	142

Isaiah

9:2	142, 143, 150–51
18:4	66
35:1–2	113
44:23	113
55:8–9	51
55:10–11	113
55:12–13	113
57:15	50
58:11	110
66:15–19	139
66:20–23	151

Jeremiah

15:19	148–49
23:23–24	141

Lamentations

3:22	149
3:31–33	149
3:31	146
3:33	146

Ezekiel

16:55	148–49

Daniel

7:10	139

Hosea

14:5	66

Scripture Index

Joel
2:28–29	136

Micah
7:8	143, 150–51

Zechariah
4:6	136

Malachi
3:2–3	138–39

NEW TESTAMENT

Matthew
6:26–30	111
7:11	45
17:4–8	57
17:11	148–49
25:31–33	143
25:40–45	144
25:41	150n22
25:46	149

Mark
9:6–8	57
9:12	148–49
10:18	45, 152
12:17	31
12:29–31	30, 31
12:44	30, 31

Luke
9:28–36	57
10:27	30
13:34	xviii, 118

John
1:1	58
1:3	58, 88
1:4	58
1:4b–5	88
1:5	151
1:9	58, 88, 143, 151
1:10	88
1:12	118
1:14	88
1:18	51
3:17–21	151
3:19–21	143
7:37–39	110
8:12	143, 151
8:58	122
13:31–35	86
14:10–23	97
15:4–15	118
21:25	119

Acts
1:8	136
3:21	148–49
17:28	47, 141
17:34	55

Romans
1:20	55
5	45
5:15	146
5:18	147, 149
5:20	147
6:4–8	118
8:11–17	136
8:11	142
8:14–17	118
8:19–22	113
8:24–39	144

Romans (continued)

8:29–30	144, 146
9:16–24	144, 146
11:32	152
11:33	109
11:36	64

1 Corinthians

1:23	119
2:1–2	119
13:8	84n26
13:12	59, 159
15:22	147
15:27–28	149
15:28	10, 152

2 Corinthians

3:9–11	142
3:16–18	142
4:6	142
4:16–18	142

Galatians

5:14	31
6:1–10	45
6:17	119

Ephesians

1:3–10	144, 146
1:4	122
1:11	149
2	118
2:10	58
3	119
4:6	10
5:5	149
5:26–27	110
6:12	143

Philippians

2:7	119

Colossians

1:15–17	58
1:17	58
1:20	149

2 Thessalonians

1:9	149

1 Timothy

2:4	149
2:4–5a	150
4:10	149
6:16	51

Titus

1:15–16	84
2:11	151
2:11–13	151

Hebrews

2:10	141
8:11	152

James

1:17	45, 142, 143, 151, 152

1 Peter

2:4–5	140

2 Peter

1:4	140
3:9	149

1 John

1:5	38, 142, 143
1:5b	150–51
2:9–11	30
2:18–28	143
3:24	86
4	30–31, 75, 85, 158
4:1–3	84
4:7	31, 83
4:8	28, 31
4:9	86
4:9–10	84
4:10–15	87
4:10	86
4:13	86
4:13–19	84
4:14	86
4:15–16	84
4:15	84, 86
4:16	30, 31, 84
4:19	30
4:19–20	30
4:20	30, 31

Revelation

20:10–15	143
20:13	144
21:6	110
21:18	151
21:21	151
21:22–26	111–12
21:23	151
21:23–26	114
21:26	151
22:5	66, 111–12
22:13	111–12
22:16	66

www.ingramcontent.com/pod-product-compliance
Lightning Source LLC
Chambersburg PA
CBHW031427150426
43191CB00006B/430